Samuel Walker 5T.

£ 1

FACTS AND RECORDS
BOOK OF
SPACE

FACTS AND RECORDS
BOOK OF
SPACE

STUART ATKINSON

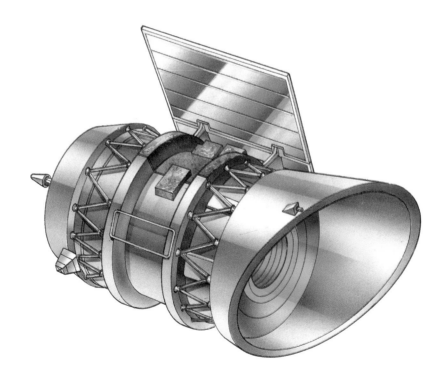

Kingfisher

Kingfisher Books, Grisewood & Dempsey Ltd,
Elsley House, 24–30 Great Titchfield Street,
London W1P 7AD

First published in paperback in 1993 by Kingfisher Books

Reprinted 1995 (with revisions)

Originally published in hardback in 1990 by Kingfisher Books
© Grisewood & Dempsey Ltd 1990

British Library Cataloguing in Publication Data
A catalogue record is available from the British Library

ISBN 1 85697 118 X

Edited by Thomas Keegan
Designed by Neville Graham
Phototypeset by Tradespools Ltd

Printed in China

The publishers would like to thank the following artists for
contributing to the book:
Chris Forsey pp. 20–25, 32–51
Lee Gibbons pp. 33, 48, 81
Jeremy Gower pp. 26–29, 72–77
Karen Johnstone (Aircraft Ltd) pp. 14/15, 18/19, 30/31, 66/67
Sebastian Quigley (Linden Artists) pp. 16/17, 52–59, 64/65
Mike Saunders pp. 12/13, 70/71, 78/79
Nick Shrewing (Garden Studio) pp. 68/69
Guy Smith (Mainline) p.35
Steve Weston (Linden Artists) pp. 60–63, 80–87.

INTRODUCTION

Ever since the first cave people gazed up at the stars in the night sky, human beings have been fascinated by the Universe around them. Today we watch on television as Space Shuttles carry men and women again and again into orbit and back to Earth. The human understanding of the Universe that has led to this achievement in space exploration has developed over hundreds of years. This book traces the amazing history of that understanding.

It describes how our knowledge of the Universe began to take shape with the invention of the telescope and with early discoveries such as Galileo's first observations of Jupiter in 1610. Since then, technology has given us bigger, better telescopes, and now satellites and computers, which astronomers use to study and observe the Universe.

This book tells how human exploration of Space began with the launch of the first artificial satellite—Sputnik 1—on October 4, 1957. This satellite was just a tiny silver ball, but it was followed by much larger spacecraft. Soon men were circling the Earth: Yuri Gagarin's first flight, in 1961, was very short, but eight years later the first man walked on the Moon. Now people live and work in space stations high above the Earth.

Robot spaceprobes have explored and photographed worlds too distant for humans to reach. In this book you can learn about their incredible discoveries, and about the exciting future plans to build bases and observatories on the Moon and to send manned expeditions to Mars!

This book will take you on a journey of discovery through the past and on into the future. Enjoy the ride!

> Abbreviations used in this book:
> mm = millimetres
> cm = centimetres
> km = kilometres
> km/h = kilometres per hour
> km^2 = square kilometres
>
> One billion = one thousand million

Contents

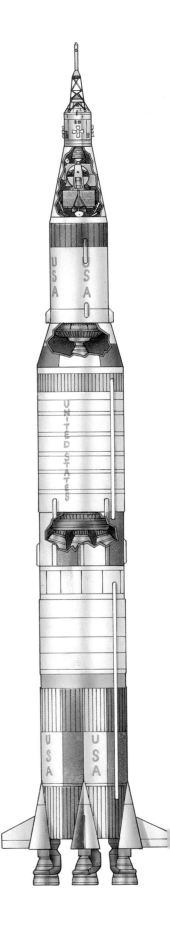

THE HEAVENS

SPACE TRAVEL

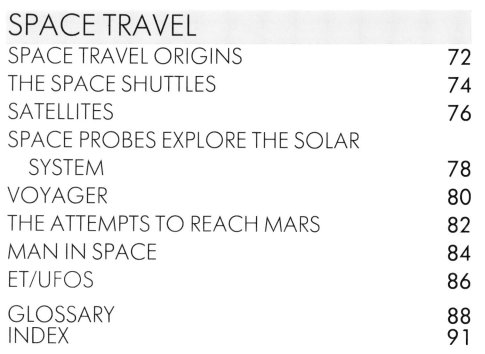

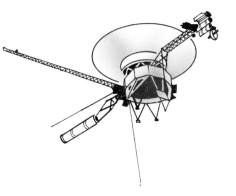

The Changing Views of the Universe

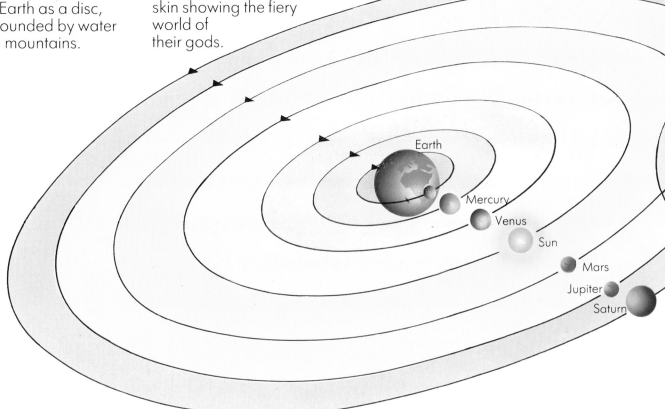

A medieval representation of Ptolemy

To the Egyptians, the heavens were their goddess Nut, while the Babylonians saw the Earth as a disc, surrounded by water and mountains.

To prehistoric people, the night sky was a huge animal hide, and stars tiny tears in the skin showing the fiery world of their gods.

Earth

Mercury

Venus

Sun

Mars

Jupiter

Saturn

The Greek Pythagoras thought the Earth was a stationary spherical globe. Aristotle used mathematics to show that the Sun and planets move around the Earth.

The Alexandrian researcher Ptolemy confirmed this view, and his Earth-centred Solar System was thus named the 'Ptolemaic Universe' or 'Ptolemaic System'.

GALILEO

Years after Copernicus, an Italian scientist, Galileo Galilei, found proof of Copernicus' theory: Jupiter had four tiny 'stars' spinning around it and Venus showed phases, changing from thin crescent to full disc. These phases could be explained only by Venus orbiting the Sun, and not the Earth!

This discovery changed our view of the Universe for ever.

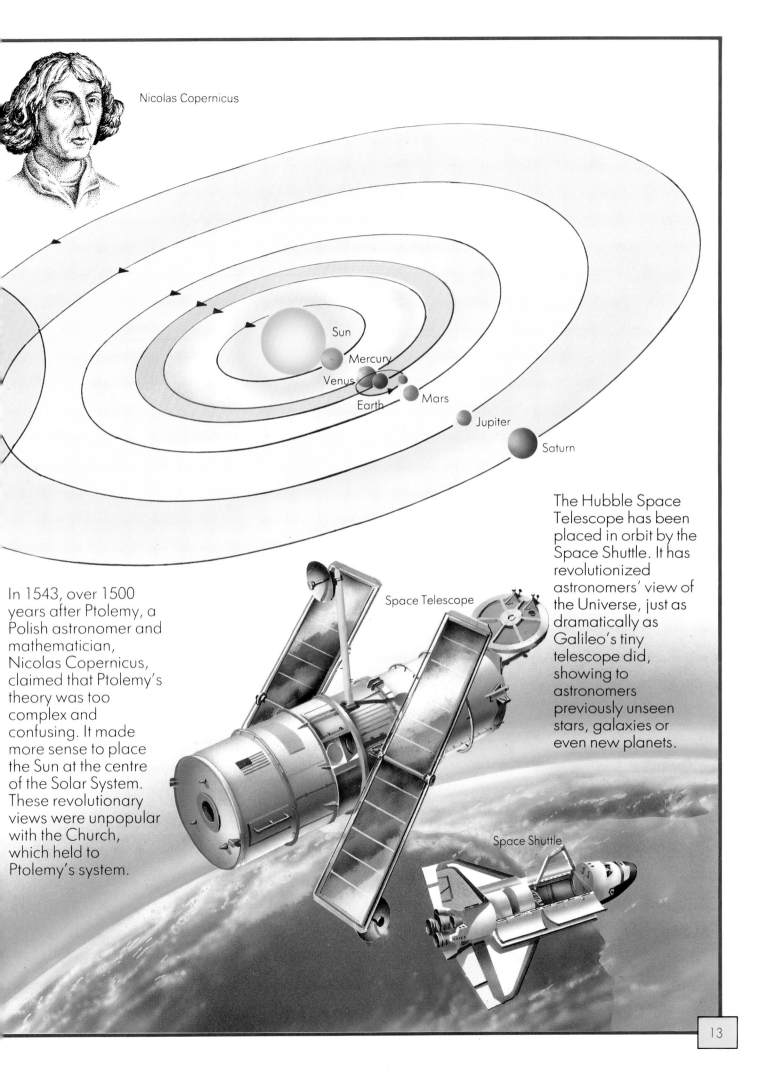

Nicolas Copernicus

Sun

Mercury

Venus

Earth

Mars

Jupiter

Saturn

In 1543, over 1500 years after Ptolemy, a Polish astronomer and mathematician, Nicolas Copernicus, claimed that Ptolemy's theory was too complex and confusing. It made more sense to place the Sun at the centre of the Solar System. These revolutionary views were unpopular with the Church, which held to Ptolemy's system.

Space Telescope

The Hubble Space Telescope has been placed in orbit by the Space Shuttle. It has revolutionized astronomers' view of the Universe, just as dramatically as Galileo's tiny telescope did, showing to astronomers previously unseen stars, galaxies or even new planets.

Space Shuttle

The Universe

The Universe is simply everything that exists. It is not just our Solar System and all the stars, galaxies and energy beyond it, but *everything* that exists anywhere. There are no limits to the Universe, although the size of telescopes limits how much we can observe from Earth. The Universe goes on and on for ever and ever. We think our Solar System is huge, and compared to the distance between the Earth and the Moon it is, but compared to the Universe, it is millions of times less important than one single cell in the massive body of a whale.

Planets

Mercury

Stars

Venus

Earth

Mars

Sun

Jupiter

Telescope

TELESCOPES

Astronomers use many different types of telescope to study the Universe. Some collect light, using large mirrors or lenses, while others collect radio waves or other types of radiation. Radio telescopes allow astronomers to study objects such as black holes, which are too dark to see. The largest telescope in the world is the Keck telescope in Hawaii, USA. It has a mirror almost 10 metres across.

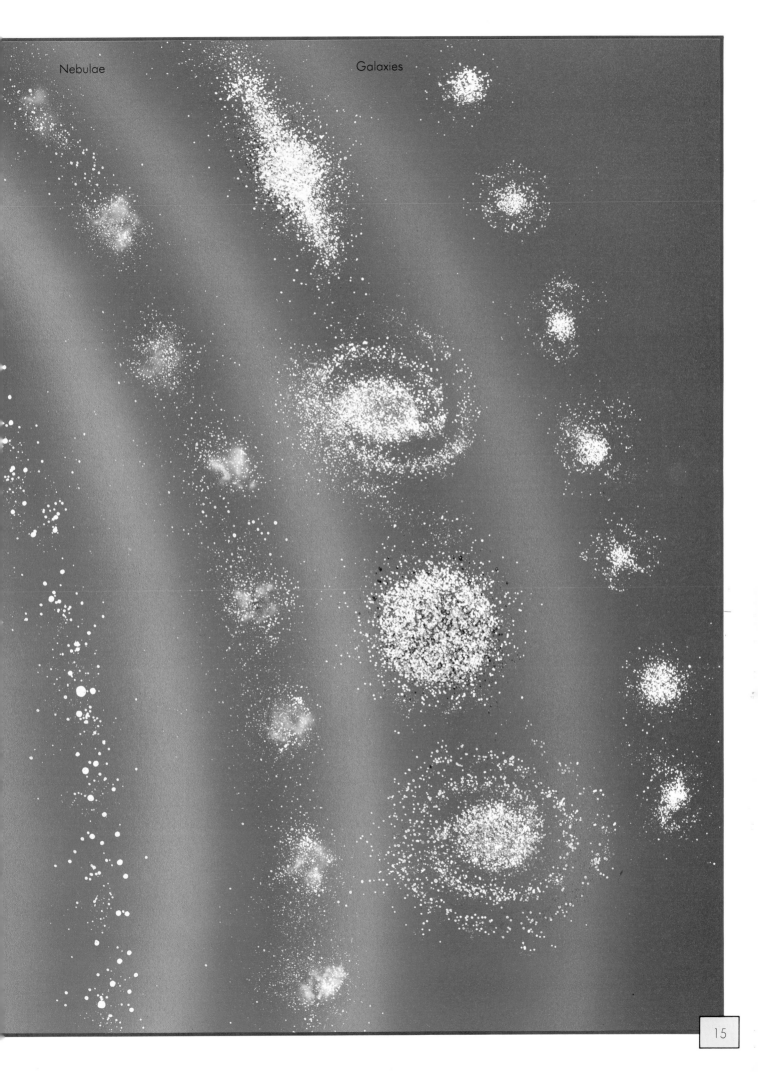

Nebulae

Galaxies

Nebulae

Galaxies

15

The Big Bang

The Universe, it is thought, was born in a massive explosion somewhere between 16 and 20 thousand million years ago, which astronomers call the 'Big Bang'. It was such a tremendous blast that comparing the Big Bang to an atomic bomb would be like comparing a cap gun to a supernova explosion. Astronomers say that nothing actually existed before the explosion; there was no space or Universe at all, and the Big Bang was the moment when Time began.

THE UNIVERSE NOW

After its violent birth, the Universe is now filled with clusters of galaxies. As older stars die, their debris reforms as gaseous nebulae, where new stars are born to take their place. The Universe is still expanding; thousands of millions of years after the Big Bang, the galaxies are all moving away from each other into space.

The infant Universe was a huge spherical fireball which expanded like an inflating bubble. During the first micro-seconds, its temperature was over 100 thousand million degrees centigrade (°C)! As it expanded it cooled, and when the Universe was three minutes old, its temperature had dropped to 'just' one thousand million degrees. Over the next millions of years, massive clouds of hydrogen began to collect and to collapse in on themselves, forming early galaxies. Later millions and millions of galaxies formed in massive clusters which make the Universe that exists today.

THE BIG CRUNCH

Can the Universe expand for ever? If the Universe is more dense than now thought, galaxies will expand a certain distance and then start to contract, ending in a Big Crunch (*below*). However, it is currently thought that the Universe will go on expanding indefinitely, with all the galaxies moving steadily away from each other.

The Earth in Space

The Earth is the only planet known to support any sort of life. Water is vital for life to exist. The Earth is unique in the Solar System for having liquid water on its surface. Most other planets are either too hot or too cold and the water either boils away or turns to ice. The Earth is 12,756 kilometres in diameter, and has a surface area of 510 million square kilometres. Land represents only three-tenths of this area. The atmosphere is 500 kilometres thick, but the dense, life-supporting part (the troposphere) is only 16 kilometres thick.

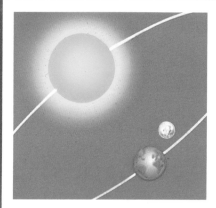

The Earth is the third planet from the Sun and orbits at a distance of 146 million kilometres.

Looking from 2000 light years away. The Sun and all its neighbours have vanished into a star cloud of many thousands of stars and cannot be made out at all.

10,000 light years away, and the star cloud becomes a tiny part of a much larger spiral arm. The Sun and its star cloud become just one of dozens of others.

The spiral arm is just one of many which are all joined at their tips to form a galaxy, 100,000 light years across. Our galaxy is called the Milky Way and altogether there are more than 200 million, million, stars in it.

Inside the Earth

The Earth has three main layers.

The solid layer we live on is the *crust*, divided into the continental region (dry land), and the oceanic region (the ocean floor). This hard, rocky layer forms 15 slabs or 'plates' which fit neatly together and move continuously.

The crust is 5 kilometres thick below the oceans and 35 kilometres thick below land.

The mantle is 2800 kilometres thick.

The *mantle* is divided into upper and lower layers. Due to the radioactive decay of its elements, it is a semi-fluid layer which is slowly turned over by convection currents rising from below.

The Earth's mass is 5.974×10^{21} (5974 with 18 noughts) tonnes.

The core is 6964 kilometres in diameter.

The Earth's *core* is divided into inner and outer layers. The temperature at the centre of the core is around 4500°C. It is made mainly of iron.

Eurasia is the largest continental land mass, covering 53,698,000 km². The smallest is Australia, which has an area of 7,686,849 km².

To study the structure of the Earth's crust in detail, Russian scientists are making the world's deepest hole. Drilling in the Kola Peninsula began in 1970, reaching 13 km in 1987. By 1990, the scientists had reached a depth of 15 km (46 times deeper than the Eiffel Tower is high).

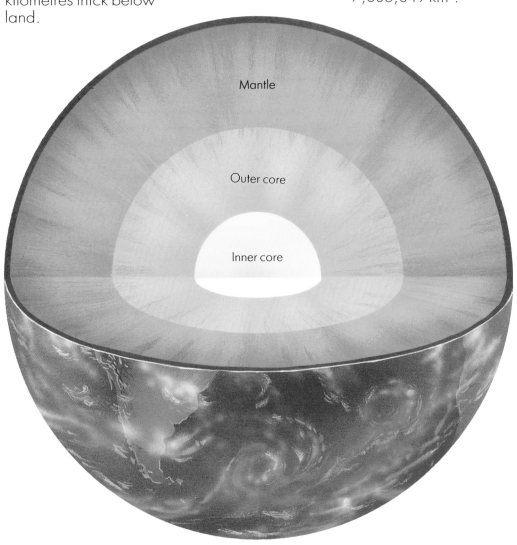

Mantle

Outer core

Inner core

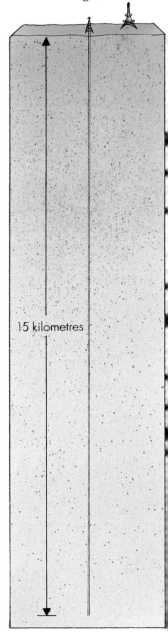

15 kilometres

Study of the movement of the 15 different crustal plates is called 'plate tectonics'. Various things happen where these plates meet:

- When an oceanic plate meets a continental plate, the former is forced down under the latter.
- Where two continental plates collide, mountain ranges such as the Himalayas are forced upwards.
- When two plates slide against each other, an unstable earthquake-prone zone is formed, (*below*).

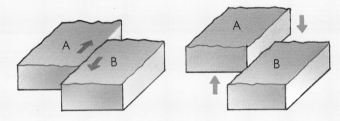

Earthquakes can be so violent that they destroy whole cities. San Francisco, situated on the infamous San Andreas Fault (the boundary between the North American and Pacific plates), was almost destroyed by a huge earthquake in 1906 and suffered damage again in October 1989 (*above*).

There are over 1300 active volcanoes on Earth, of which 77 are in Indonesia.

Volcanoes occur when molten magma is forced up from below the crust and red hot lava spills out from the cone-shaped peaks. Some volcanoes may erupt regularly without much damage, but others cause massive devastation. The volcano on the island of Krakatoa erupted in 1883 with the power of 36 hydrogen bombs, destroying 163 villages, killing 36,380 people and hurling rocks over 50 kilometres into the air.

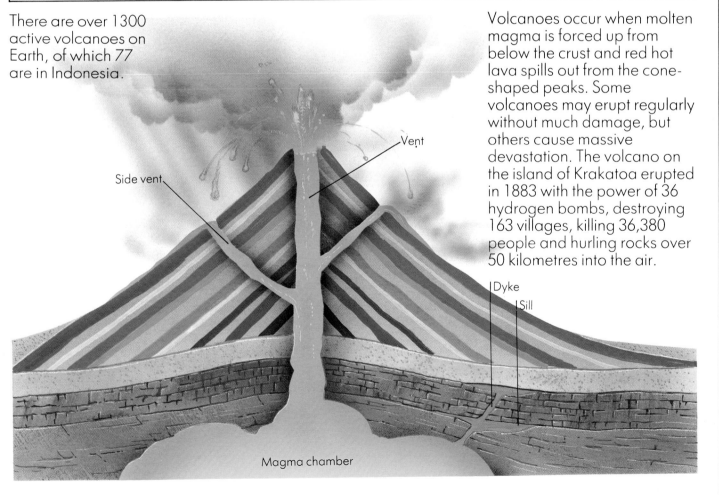

Side vent

Vent

Dyke

Sill

Magma chamber

The Oceans

More than two thirds of Earth's surface is covered in water, distinguishing it from all other planets. Earth's oceans not only help to cool the planet, but also have provided humans with fish for thousands of years.

We know less about the undersea world than about the surface of Mars. The ocean floor is a violent, ever-changing place, with cracks or fractures from which scalding-hot water blasts towards the surface, and undersea volcanoes and mountains, the highest of which make Everest seem like a small hill. Deep shadowy trenches descend for many kilometres, hiding creatures we can only imagine.

Atlantic

Trench

Mountain ridges

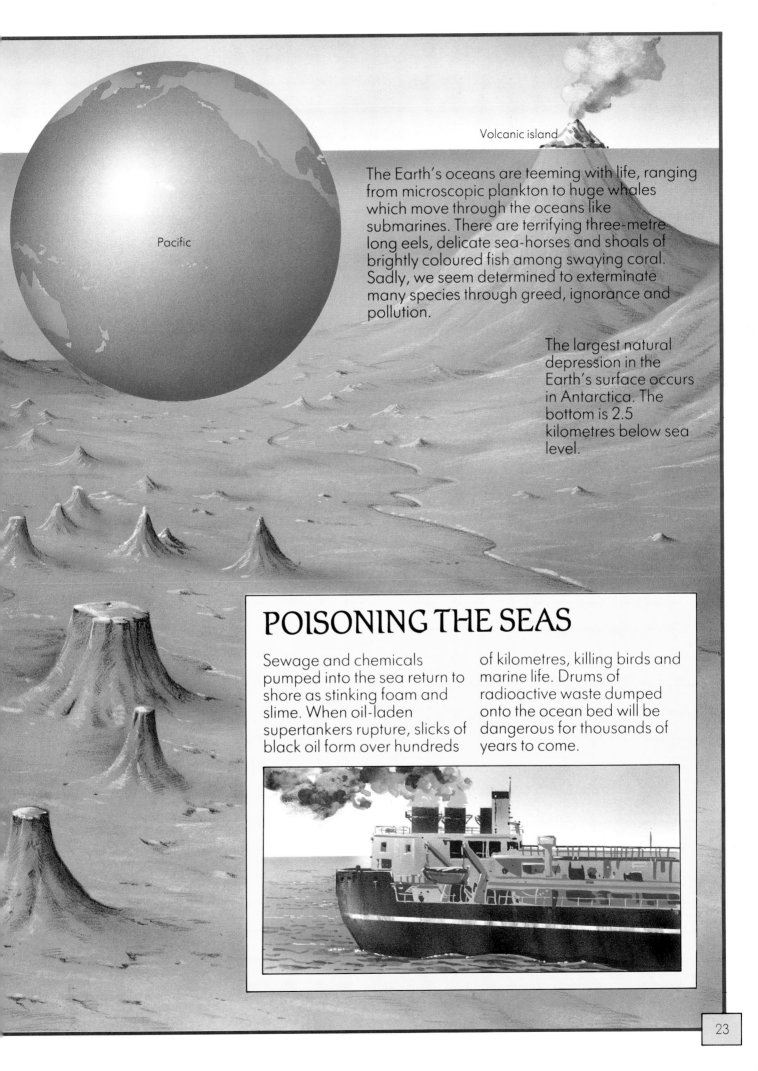

Volcanic island

Pacific

The Earth's oceans are teeming with life, ranging from microscopic plankton to huge whales which move through the oceans like submarines. There are terrifying three-metre long eels, delicate sea-horses and shoals of brightly coloured fish among swaying coral. Sadly, we seem determined to exterminate many species through greed, ignorance and pollution.

The largest natural depression in the Earth's surface occurs in Antarctica. The bottom is 2.5 kilometres below sea level.

POISONING THE SEAS

Sewage and chemicals pumped into the sea return to shore as stinking foam and slime. When oil-laden supertankers rupture, slicks of black oil form over hundreds of kilometres, killing birds and marine life. Drums of radioactive waste dumped onto the ocean bed will be dangerous for thousands of years to come.

The Moon

The deepest crater on the Moon is 'Newton'. It is almost nine kilometres deep!

The diameter of the Earth is 12,756 kilometres.
The diameter of the Moon is 3476 kilometres and its surface area is not much bigger than that of Australia. As it is relatively so large some astronomers think the Earth and Moon should together be termed a 'Double Planet'.

It is not known exactly how the Moon was formed, but one theory is that soon after the Earth's formation, around 4.6 thousand million years ago, an object the size of Mars smashed into it. The collision sent a massive shower of debris into orbit, which collided and gradually fused into a large solid object. Heat from the constant collisions kept the Moon's surface molten; heavier elements such as iron sank to the centre and the lighter elements floated upwards to form a solid crust.

The Moon takes exactly the same length of time to make one complete orbit of the Earth as it does to revolve once on its own axis: 27.3 days. This is why we always see the same face of the Moon.

Sea of Showers

Ocean of Storms

Sea of Clouds

Sea of Humours

Earth

Moon

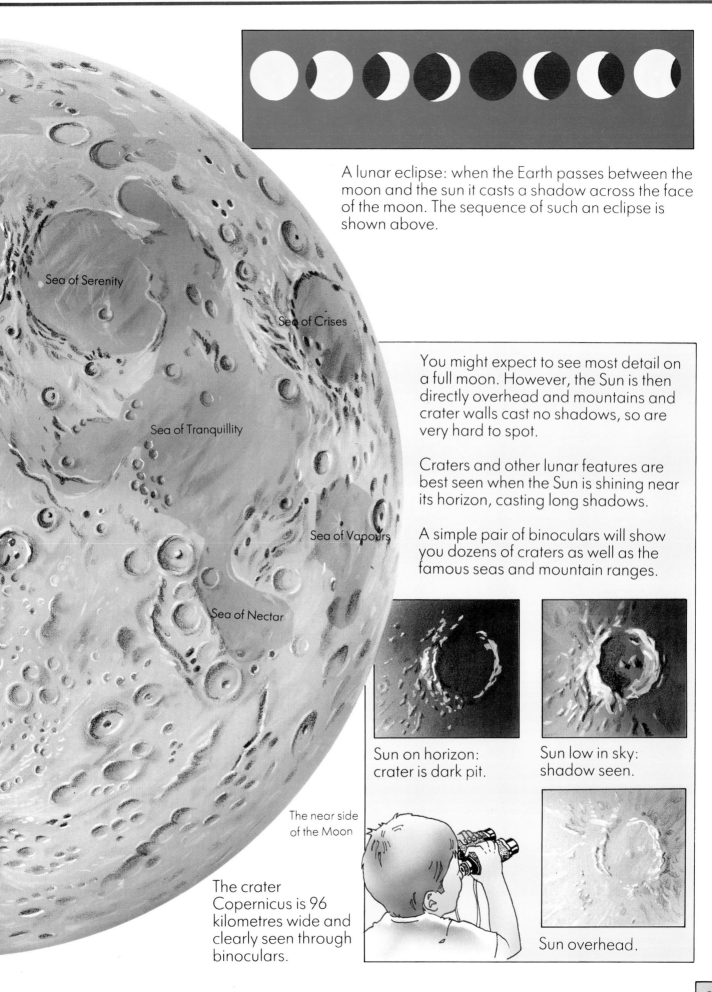

A lunar eclipse: when the Earth passes between the moon and the sun it casts a shadow across the face of the moon. The sequence of such an eclipse is shown above.

Sea of Serenity

Sea of Crises

Sea of Tranquillity

Sea of Vapours

Sea of Nectar

You might expect to see most detail on a full moon. However, the Sun is then directly overhead and mountains and crater walls cast no shadows, so are very hard to spot.

Craters and other lunar features are best seen when the Sun is shining near its horizon, casting long shadows.

A simple pair of binoculars will show you dozens of craters as well as the famous seas and mountain ranges.

Sun on horizon: crater is dark pit.

Sun low in sky: shadow seen.

The near side of the Moon

Sun overhead.

The crater Copernicus is 96 kilometres wide and clearly seen through binoculars.

Getting to the Moon

The Soviet Union was the first nation to reach the Moon with its unmanned robot *Luna* probes in 1959. The first probe, Luna 1, sent back information, but no pictures. Ten months later Luna 3 took pictures of the Moon's previously unseen Far Side. On 31 January 1966 the 9th Luna probe landed on the Moon and returned the first pictures from the surface. Luna probes also gathered small samples of lunar soil and analysed them.

The Saturn 5 was split in several different section or 'stages'. After launch the first stage engines carried the rocket high into the atmosphere un their fuel ran out just 15 seconds later. The second stage then took over, its engines taking the spacecraft almost in orbit. When its fuel ran out too, the third stage engines placed the craf in a 'parking orbit' abov the Earth while the astronauts checked thei equipment. Then the thi stage rocket fired again to send the Apollo spacecraft towards the Moon.

The Saturn 5 rocket carried two different Apollo spacecraft. On the top of the rocket was the conical Command Module, which carried the astronauts up into space. The Command Module was stacked on top of the Lunar Module a spidery craft made to take the astronauts dow to the Moon's surface.

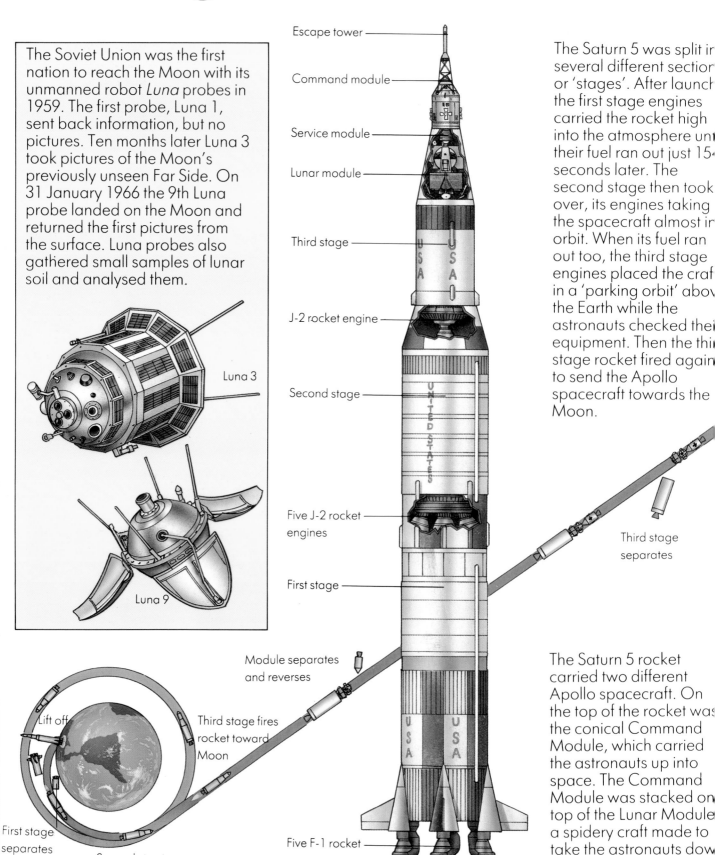

Luna 3

Luna 9

Escape tower

Command module

Service module

Lunar module

Third stage

J-2 rocket engine

Second stage

Five J-2 rocket engines

First stage

Five F-1 rocket engines

Third stage separates

Module separates and reverses

Third stage fires rocket toward Moon

Lift off

First stage separates

Second stage separates

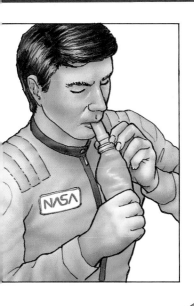

The Apollo astronauts lived in cramped conditions, surrounded by hundreds of instruments and dials. They ate food from small tubes, adding water to make a meal later described as 'mashed mouse'!

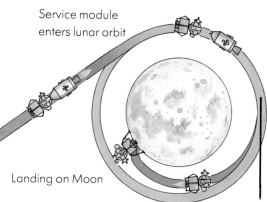

Service module enters lunar orbit

Landing on Moon

Lunar module separates

The first attempt to send a probe to the Moon was a complete failure. The Able 1 probe, launched by the United States on 1 August 1958 never even reached the Moon.

During the flight the Command Module was joined – or 'docked' – to the Lunar Module. Once both the craft were in lunar orbit, two of the crew entered the Lunar Module. The third astronaut remained in the Command Module. The two craft then separated, leaving the Command Module in orbit while the Lunar Module descended to the surface.

The descent was partly controlled by computer, making the engine fire in short bursts to slow the Lunar Module down. Just minutes from the surface, however, the pilot took over, skilfully guiding his spindly craft away from large craters and unexpected fields of boulders.

Lunar module

The Saturn 5 rocket which took men to the Moon stood over 120 metres tall. The gleaming white rocket's mighty engines produced a thrust of over 3,402,000 kilograms.

The Surface of the Moon

The Lunar Module flew for the very first time on the Apollo 9 mission in March 1969.

One of the astronauts' most important tasks was to bring back samples of lunar rock and soil for analysis and study. They took interesting samples, using special drills to bore below the surface and take long cylindrical rock samples.

The Apollo 11 mission cost over $355 million!

Because of their limited air supply, the astronauts could not spend long away from the Lunar Module. NASA gave the Apollo 15, 16 and 17 crews Lunar Rovers so they could travel farther. These 'beach buggies', powered by electric batteries, had a large antenna for communicating with the Earth.

The astronauts also set up various scientific experiments on the Moon, left to continue working after their departure.

Lunar module

MOONDUST

Commander Neil Armstrong found the Moon surface solid and safe, with a layer of fine, powdery dust, which stuck to his boots 'like wet sand'. There is no air on the Moon to create winds, so the footprints will remain for ever.

Siesmometer

The Moon is a barren, lifeless world, and without an atmosphere the sky is black and cold. Because it is smaller than Earth the horizon seems very close, and Apollo astronauts reported how they felt the ground curving away below them. The horizon shows rolling hills, and the grey/brown landscape is scattered with boulders and rocks.

On the Apollo 14 mission in 1971, astronaut Alan Shepard used a soil-sample scoop as a golf club and sent a rock shooting across the surface. The Apollo astronauts also enjoyed exercising in the low gravity.

Because no air softens the Sun's light, all shadows on the Moon are a deep black and have sharp edges. The Sun shines brilliantly by day, and the stars by night. The Earth from the Moon resembles a blue marble, frosted over with swirls of white cloud, with phases just like the Moon.

Lunar rover

Return to Earth

After completing their tasks, the Apollo astronauts returned to the Lunar Module, fired the engines on the Ascent Stage and took off. They only had one chance for this to work. Had it failed they would have stayed there and died. The Lunar Module docked with the orbiting Command Module, the landing team returned to the Command Module, and the craft separated.

The conical Command Module separated from its engine section in orbit and began to drop down into the atmosphere.

All the early American space missions ended with a 'splashdown' in the ocean. When the Command Module hit the water, inflatable cushions kept it afloat until a helicopter came to rescue the astronauts.

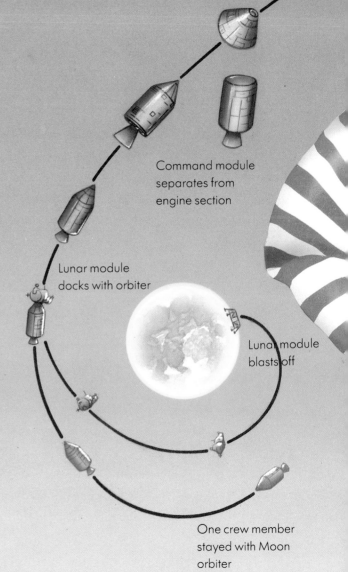

Command module turns around for re-entry – and splashdown

Command module separates from engine section

Lunar module docks with orbiter

Lunar module blasts off

One crew member stayed with Moon orbiter

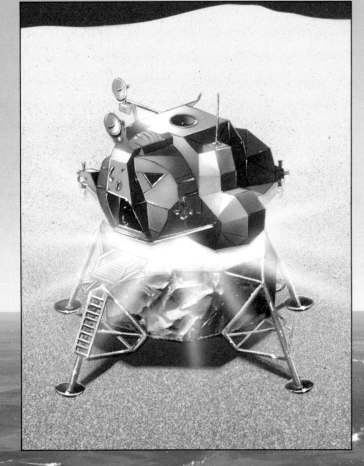

As the Command Module dropped through the atmosphere, the friction of air molecules rubbing against its base created heat. Had the base not been covered with a special heat shield, it would have burnt up like a meteor.

MOONROCK

The Moon rocks collected from different sites gave scientists a lot of information. They contained very little oxygen or potassium, but did contain common elements such as calcium, titanium and aluminium. Tests on tiny fragments of green Moon rock revealed an age of roughly 4 thousand million years. The youngest rock sample was returned by the crew of Apollo 15; it was just 3.2 thousand million years old.

The Solar System

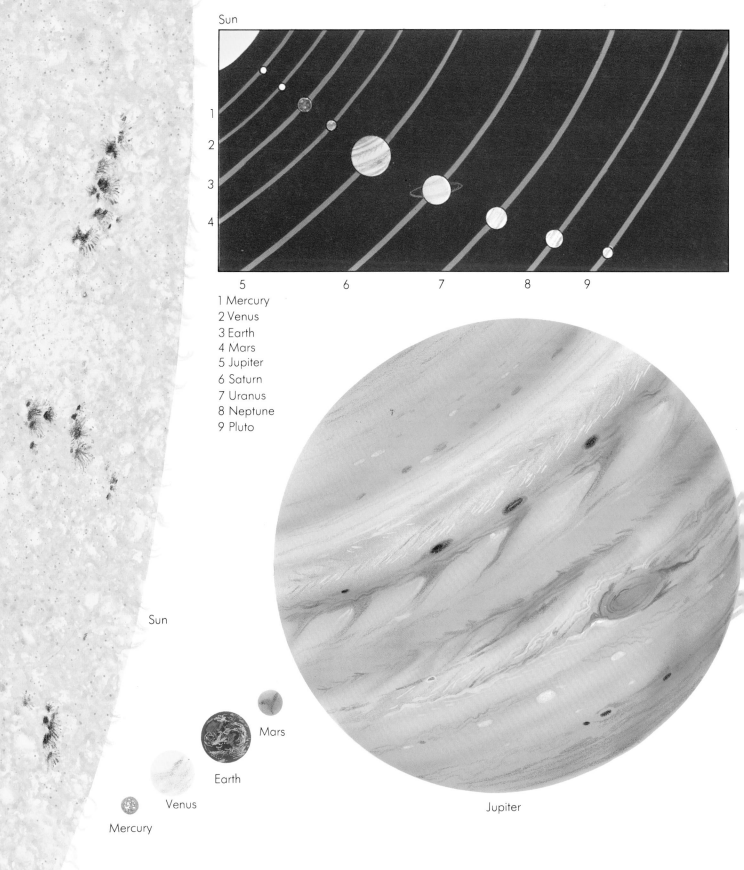

Sun

1 Mercury
2 Venus
3 Earth
4 Mars
5 Jupiter
6 Saturn
7 Uranus
8 Neptune
9 Pluto

Sun

Mercury

Venus

Earth

Mars

Jupiter

Neptune

Uranus

Saturn

NOTE: 'Length of day'
is equivalent to time
taken to make one
complete rotation.

MERCURY

Diameter	– 4880 km
Size compared to Earth	– 0.4x
Length of year	– 88 days
Length of day	– 58 days 16 hours
Distance from SUN	– 57.9 million km

VENUS

Diameter	– 12104 km
Size compared to Earth	– 0.95x
Length of year	– 224.7 days
Length of day	– 243 days (Retrograde)
Distance from SUN	– 108 million km

EARTH

Diameter	– 12756 km
Size compared to Earth	– 1x
Length of year	– 365.25 days
Length of day	– 23h 56m
Distance from SUN	– 150 million km

MARS

Diameter	– 6787 km
Size compared to Earth	– 0.5x
Length of year	– 687 days
Length of day	– 24h 37m
Distance from SUN	– 228 million km

JUPITER

Diameter	– 142600 km
Size compared to Earth	– 11x
Length of year	– 11.84 years
Length of day	– 9h 50m
Distance from SUN	– 778 million km

SATURN

Diameter	– 120200 km
Size compared to Earth	– 9x
Length of year	– 29.46 years
Length of day	– 10h 14m
Distance from SUN	– 1427 million km

URANUS

Diameter	– 51800 km
Size compared to Earth	– 4x
Length of year	– 84 years
Length of day	– 17h (Retrograde)
Distance from SUN	– 2869 million km

NEPTUNE

Diameter	– 49500 km
Size compared to Earth	– 3.8x
Length of year	– 164.8 days
Length of day	– 18h
Distance from SUN	– 4497 million km

PLUTO

Diameter	– 2400 km
Size compared to Earth	– 0.18x
Length of year	– 248 years
Length of day	– 6d 9h
Distance from SUN	– 5900 million km

The Sun

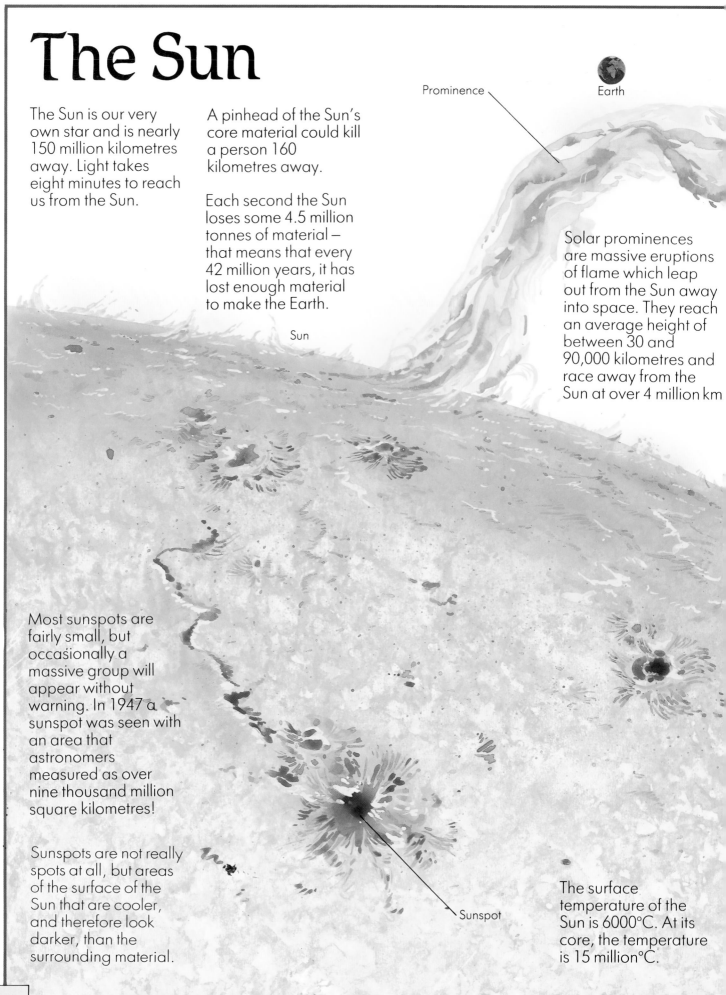

The Sun is our very own star and is nearly 150 million kilometres away. Light takes eight minutes to reach us from the Sun.

A pinhead of the Sun's core material could kill a person 160 kilometres away.

Each second the Sun loses some 4.5 million tonnes of material – that means that every 42 million years, it has lost enough material to make the Earth.

Sun

Prominence

Earth

Solar prominences are massive eruptions of flame which leap out from the Sun away into space. They reach an average height of between 30 and 90,000 kilometres and race away from the Sun at over 4 million km

Most sunspots are fairly small, but occasionally a massive group will appear without warning. In 1947 a sunspot was seen with an area that astronomers measured as over nine thousand million square kilometres!

Sunspots are not really spots at all, but areas of the surface of the Sun that are cooler, and therefore look darker, than the surrounding material.

Sunspot

The surface temperature of the Sun is 6000°C. At its core, the temperature is 15 million°C.

The Sun has several layers, but is made entirely out of super-hot gases. It is over 109 times wider than the Earth.

A Solar prominence sends millions of tonnes of solar material hurtling out into space – enough to incinerate the Earth.

A solar flare is a burst of deadly radiation. When its energy reaches Earth, it can disrupt radio and TV signals, and causes the Northern Lights.

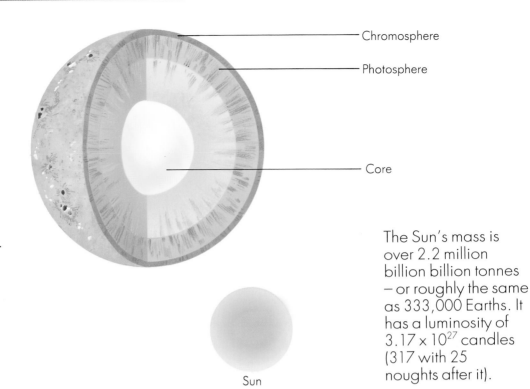

Chromosphere

Photosphere

Core

Sun

The Sun's mass is over 2.2 million billion billion tonnes – or roughly the same as 333,000 Earths. It has a luminosity of 3.17×10^{27} candles (317 with 25 noughts after it).

SOLAR ECLIPSES

Total eclipse seen here

A total solar eclipse reveals the Sun's corona

A total solar eclipse happens when the Moon passes directly between the Sun and the Earth. The Sun disappears behind the Moon's dark disc leaving only the Sun's outer corona visible. Scientists can learn much from this outer layer. It is where the huge solar flares erupt sending violent bursts of radiation out in to space. Eclipses happen somewhere every six months.

Mercury

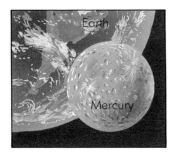

Earth

Mercury

Mercury has a large iron core, 3600 kilometres in diameter, about the size of the Moon.

Mercury is a small world; its equatorial diameter of 4880 kilometres is roughly one-third of Earth's and smaller than Jupiter's moon Ganymede!

From Earth Mercury appears as a bright 'star' visible for only a short time, either just before sunrise or after sunset. It is very hard to see because it is close to the Sun and is easily lost in the solar glare. It usually appears flashing close to the horizon.

Mariner 10 was 45.5 centimetres high, and a little over 1.2 metres wide. It carried instruments to measure the intensity of magnetic energy, and telescopes which could 'see' ultra-violet radiation. The Mariner 10 probe had also journeyed to Venus, but its most exciting discovery was the cratered, inhospitable world of Mercury. It took over 8000 photographs.

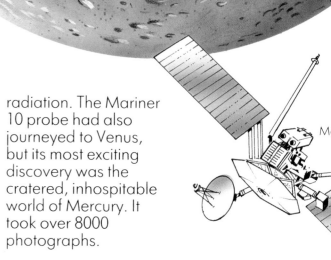

Because Mercury is much closer to the Sun than Earth, the Sun in Mercury's sky appears over twice the size that we see it.

From a distance it looks like our own Moon and is a dark grey, lifeless ball of rock, covered in craters and mountains. As on the Moon, the youngest craters have streaks of bright material spreading out from them.

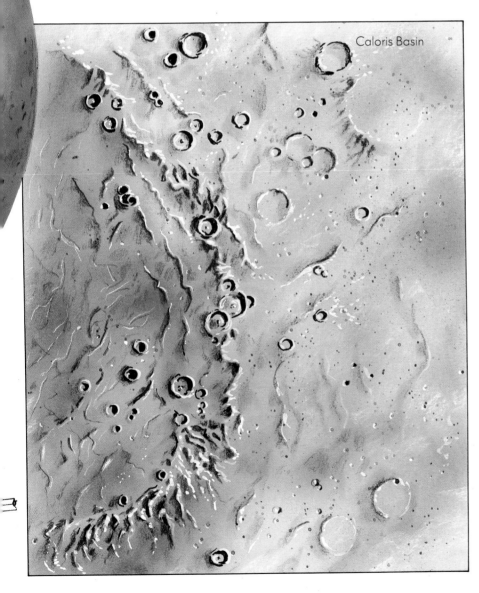

Caloris Basin

Caloris Basin is the largest feature on the surface of Mercury, with a diameter of 1300 kilometres. It was formed when an object 100 kilometres wide smashed into the planet at a speed of 512,000 km/h many millions of years ago. Molten material flooded out over the shattered surface, forming concentric rings. The basin now looks like a bulls-eye.

Formation of Caloris Basin

Venus

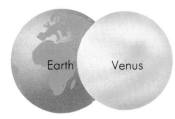

Earth Venus

Venus has an equatorial diameter of 12,104 kilometres, just 652 kilometres smaller than Earth.

Venus was named after the Roman goddess of love. In the night sky it resembles a brilliant blue-white star. Venus is visible for a few hours before sunrise or after sunset at certain times of the year.

The first probe to transmit data from the surface of Venus was the Soviet Venera 7 probe. In December 1970 it survived for 23 minutes.

Earth

Venus' dense atmosphere means that we cannot see its actual surface directly. Between 1978 and 1980 the American Pioneer-Venus space probe mapped nearly 98% of the planet's surface using radar.

Radar map of Venus

Pictures from the Pioneer space probe showed that Venus looks like a huge ball of yellow-grey smoke. It has a dense, opaque atmosphere of carbon dioxide and clouds of sulphuric acid that hide its surface features. Within this atmosphere, all that are visible are vague 'Y'-shaped features revolving around the planet. Venus spins from east to west, the opposite direction to Earth; and so, on Venus the Sun rises in the west and sets in the east.

MAGELLAN

The Magellan space probe, launched by the Space Shuttle, has mapped the surface of Venus in great detail using radar. It has revealed craters, volcanoes and mountains invisible until now.

Magellan probe

Venus' orange clouds hide a world of molten, shimmering rocks and fierce winds. Its surface temperature is almost 500°C, even hotter than Mercury.

The atmosphere is so dense that its surface pressure is the same as Earth's water pressure on an ocean bed. Such intense pressure has pulverized and crushed surface rocks. The sulphurous atmosphere produces lethal sulphuric acid rain!

Mars

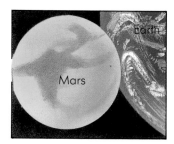

Mars   Earth

Mars is a small world; its equatorial diameter of 6787 kilometres – roughly half the size of Earth. However, because Mars has no oceans, it has the same land area as our own planet.

Early observations of Mars with telescopes showed just a few dark markings on its orange globe – partly because the early telescopes were of poor quality, and partly the planet's atmosphere obscures interesting surface details. More advanced telescopes showed details such as polar caps. Astronomers – especially Percival Lowall – claimed to see dozens of straight lines on the surface and said these were irrigation canals.

However, in 1964 the first space probe to photograph Mars successfully, Mariner 4, proved the canals did not exist. Mars

was revealed as a dead, desolate world of craters, valleys, dust dunes and extinct volcanoes. In colour photographs from later probes, it looks like a scarred, pockmarked orange, with a few wisps of silvery cloud and shining white polar caps.

Mars

The massive Valles Marineris, or 'Mariner Valley' was discovered by the Mariner 9 space probe in 1971–72.

Phobos

Phobos orbits at just
5982 km. In the
Martian sky it appears
about half the size of
our Moon.

Deimos

Deimos is over
23,000 kilometres
from Mars and would
appear from there to
be a very bright star.

Olympus Mons

VIKING LANDERS

Viking 1, launched on
20 August 1975,
reached Mars in ten
months. Viking 2,
launched a month
later, reached the Red
Planet three months
after Viking 1. The
orbiters took
photographs while the
Landers descended to
the surface.
Their photographs
showed a Martian
landscape of stony
desert, with jagged
rocks stretching to
the horizon.

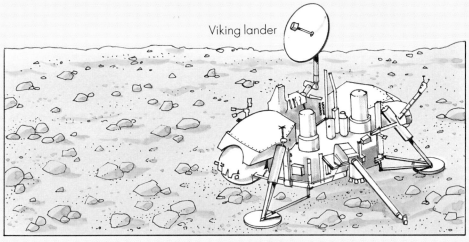
Viking lander

Study of a Viking 1 orbiter
photograph in 1976 revealed an
apparently human face with eyes,
nose and mouth, framed by an
'Egyptian' head-dress. However,
the 'face' is really just a mesa, or
raised platform of rock, and its
carved appearance is only a
coincidence.

Astronomers suggest
that Phobos and
Deimos are probably
captured asteroids,
because of their size.

People seeing Mars'
desert-red colour
might think it is hot,
but Viking found that
it was very cold and
dry, with an average
temperature of −23°C.

Jupiter

Jupiter

Earth

Jupiter is the largest planet in the Solar System. Its equatorial diameter is 142,600 kilometres, over 11 times greater Earth's!

Jupiter appears in the night sky as a bright white star; through a telescope it looks like a yellow-white disc, its face marked with several horizontal belts of dark cloud. Seen from orbit the planet's bloated, orange-brown disc is streaked with dozens of moving cloud belts of different colours.

If you were to represent the Earth as a one penny piece, Jupiter would be as large as a plate.

In 1994 pieces of a comet called Shoemaker Levy-9 smashed into Jupiter, leaving huge, dark marks.

The four largest and most important satellites of Jupiter are those discovered by Galileo in 1610 and known as the 'Galilean' moons: Ganymede, Io, Callisto and Europa.

Our Moon

Ganymede

Callisto

Voyager 1 revealed a faint, very thin and totally unexpected ring around Jupiter. This had never been seen from Earth because it was so faint compared to the brilliance of the planet. The whole ring system is approximately 5920 kilometres wide, and just one kilometre thick.

The layers of the atmosphere

Water and ice crystals

Ammonium hydrosulphide and ammonia crystals

Gaseous hydrogen

Jupiter has no solid surface on which astronauts could land. Astronomers call it a 'Gas Giant', made entirely from different forms of gas.

The surface we see from orbit is merely the planet's highest atmosphere layer. Hidden beneath the shifting clouds is a huge ocean, and beneath that a dense core approximately the size of Earth. The clouds are made out of gases like hydrogen, helium, methane and ammonia.

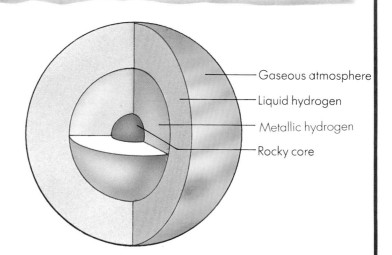

- Gaseous atmosphere
- Liquid hydrogen
- Metallic hydrogen
- Rocky core

Europa

Io

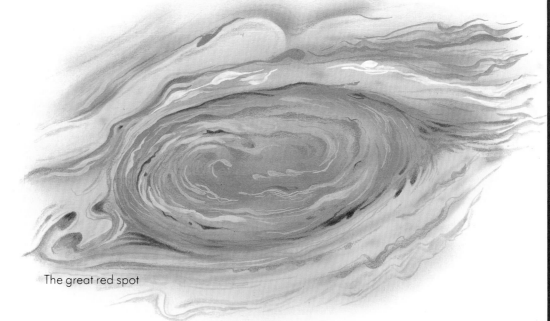

The great red spot

THE RED SPOT

The most dramatic feature on Jupiter is the Great Red Spot, which has been observed by astronomers for hundreds of years. Only when the

Voyager space probes explored Jupiter did we come to understand that it is a massive revolving storm, over three times the size of Earth.

Saturn

Saturn is the second largest planet in our Solar System with an equatorial diameter of 120,200 kilometres. It is more than nine times bigger than Earth!

Voyager

Beneath the atmosphere, an ocean of molecular liquid hydrogen enfolds a shell of metallic hydrogen. The centre is a rocky core the same size as Earth.

Saturn

Just like Jupiter, Saturn has a family of orbiting satellites, mostly made of ice. Saturn has 18 known satellites; four are illustrated here. The closest of these moons to Saturn is Mimas, a ball of ice just 512 kilometres wide orbiting the planet at a distance of 185,540 kilometres.

Dione, which lies 377,420 kilometres from Saturn is 1120 kilometres wide, or one third the width of our Moon.

Titan, with a diameter of 5120 kilometres, is bigger even than Mercury. It is the only moon in the solar system to have an atmosphere, made mainly of nitrogen.

Tethys has a diameter of just over 1000 kilometres and orbits its parent planet at a distance of 294,700 kilometres.

Next moon out is Enceladus. Enceladus is just 110 kilometres wider than Mimas, and orbits at a distance of 238,000 kilometres.

Dione

With a large telescope, you can see Saturn's rings clearly, and also the vague markings on its surface.

Tethys

Like Jupiter, Saturn is a Gas Giant, and its disc is noticeably flattened at the poles to resemble a squashed tennis ball. This is because the planet spins so fast that centrifugal force makes the equator bulge outwards.

From Earth three bands of Saturn's rings can be seen. Voyager found the bands to be made from thousands, if not millions, of very thin rings.

Because Saturn is tilted on its axis, we occasionally pass through the plane of its rings, either dropping below or rising above the line of the rings. Over a period of time we see Saturn's rings grow bigger and bigger until they are wide open (A–C). Then they appear to grow thinner and finally vanish altogether (D–E). The cycle then repeats itself (F–I). The process takes about 29 years.

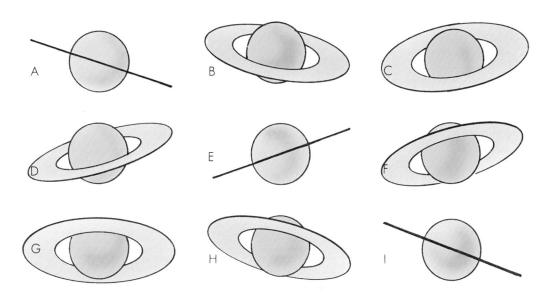

Mimas

Enceladus

SATURN'S RINGS

Saturn's rings are not solid, but more like a blizzard in orbit around the planet's equator. They are made up of particles of rock and ice of different sizes. There are countless thousands of rings made from billions of ring particles, each orbiting the planet like a miniature moon. The impressive rings are very insubstantial, possibly only one kilometre thick.

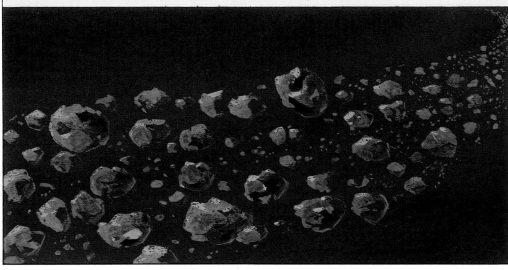

Uranus

Uranus is tipped over, so that it rolls around the Sun on its side like a barrel. Its poles are at an angle of 98 degrees to its orbit.

Saturn

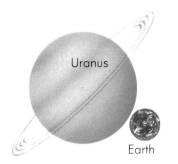

Uranus

Earth

Uranus lies 2869 million kilometres from the Sun. It's diameter is 51,800 kilometres – four times that of Earth, but only half that of Saturn.

Uranus is so far away that it appears only faintly in the night sky. A telescope shows a tiny blurred green disc, with very vague surface markings.

The Voyager 2 has shown Uranus to be green, because its atmosphere – (mostly hydrogen and helium) – contains methane gas. Methane absorbs red light, so all the light rebounding off the planet becomes a green-blue colour. Voyager 2 discovered that Uranus' atmosphere is hidden beneath a deep blanket of haze, like Saturn's moon Titan. The only atmospheric features they found were a few cloud belts and some fast-moving, high altitude streaks of cloud.

William Herschel, who discovered Uranus first wanted to call it Georgius Sidus after the King of England, George III. This was not a popular choice and the planet was finally named after the first sky god of Greek mythology.

The temperature of Uranus' cloud tops is estimated to be −216°C.

Because Uranus rotates on its side the equator actually receives less sunlight than the poles.

Uranus

Voyager 2 flew past Uranus in 1986. It made many importa... discoveries including nine moons which h... never been seen be... and which were na... after characters in Shakespeare's plays

It is not known why Uranus rotates on its side rather than in an upright position. This not its only orbital eccentricity; like Ven... it spins about its axis the opposite directio... to the other planets, clockwise.

THE MOONS OF URANUS

Ariel

Umbriel

Titania

Ariel is a very dark world, with many craters and deep, gouge-like trenches running across its surface.

Umbriel, virtually the same size as Ariel, has a charcoal-grey surface pitted with craters, some very recent.

Titania is the largest of the major moons, with a diameter of 1590 kilometres is almost half the size of our own Moon.

The drawings above are not to scale. The diameters of the moons are:
Ariel 1160 km
Umbriel 1170 km
Titania 1590 km
Miranda 480 km
Oberon 1525 km.
Miranda has ice cliffs on its surface that could be 20 km high.

Uranus was the first planet discovered by astronomers. All the nearer planets were visible to the naked eye. Uranus was discovered by William Herschel on 13 March 1781, while observing the constellation Gemini.

William Herschel

William Herschel constructed what was in the 1780s the largest telescope ever built. It had an aperture of 1.2 metres but was so large it was difficult to use. Herschel usually used a smaller 47 cm telescope.

On 10 March 1977, a team of astronomers were preparing to observe the passage of a star behind the disc of the planet Uranus (an occultation). Half an hour before the occultation was due to begin, the star 'winked' unexpectedly. Later the star winked again on the opposite side of the planet. The astronomers calculated that Uranus must have rings, which had temporarily blocked out the star.

Uranus's rings

Neptune

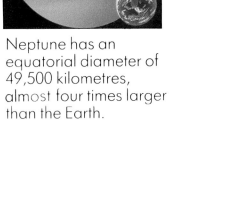

Neptune

Earth

Neptune has an equatorial diameter of 49,500 kilometres, almost four times larger than the Earth.

Voyager 2 passed within 4900 kilometres of the upper clouds covering Neptune's surface.

Voyager 2 was the first probe to visit the outer planets. Little was known about Neptune before it arrived.

Neptune's existence was inferred long before it was seen. Uranus orbits eccentrically and 19th century mathematicians calculated this to be caused by a planet lying outside Uranus.

Neptune

Voyager 2's cameras revealed a dynamic and stunningly beautiful planet. It was powder-blue in colour, because the methane in its atmosphere absorbs red light, and like Jupiter, had a huge oval hurricane system. It also had streamers of bright white cloud, several smaller storm systems, and a broad band of cloud around its south pole. The clouds and other atmospheric features travel at up to 1440 km/h.

Triton is Neptune's largest moon, just 2720 kilometres wide – smaller even than our own Moon! It is an icy world of frozen methane and nitrogen, which has turned pink with exposure to sunlight. Its fascinating surface of craters, valleys, ridges and frozen methane lakes may also contain erupting volcanoes.

Triton

oyager made many
ascinating
iscoveries at
leptune, changing
istronomers' views of
he planet for ever.

We now think
Neptune's atmosphere
overs an 'ocean' of
iquid methane and
ce slush surrounding
rocky core.

The Scooter, a wedge
of blue-white cloud,
aces around the
planet on a 'track' half
way between its
Great Dark Spot and
he south pole.

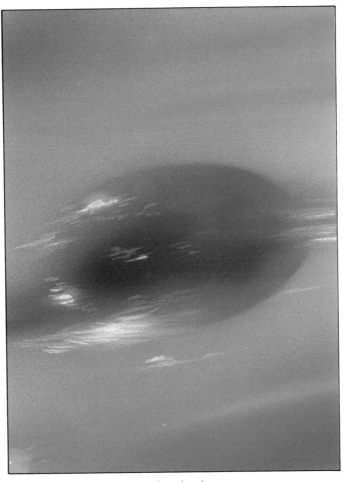

Voyager 2 photographed a huge rotating storm on
Neptune, called the Great Dark Spot. It had
streaks of bright cloud shining above it. Unlike
Jupiter's Great Red Spot, it does not appear to be
permanent; photos taken in 1995 by the Hubble
Space Telescope showed that it had vanished!

Voyager detected
shimmering curtains of
light 'aurorae' on
Neptune. Like the
aurorae seen on Earth
(the 'Northern Lights')
and Jupiter, they are
caused by particles
from the Sun
interacting with the
planet's magnetic
field.

Voyager 2 discovered
six new moons in orbit
around Neptune.
They are very small,
with diameters less
than 500 kilometres,
and resemble the tiny
icy satellites of Saturn
and Uranus.
Photographs taken
through Voyager's
cameras showed
craters on their cold,
dark surfaces.

It was believed that Neptune
had several partial rings or
'ring-arcs' going around it,
not a complete ring system.
Voyager 2 discovered the
arcs were in fact *three*
complete rings. The
outermost two are the
brightest (still much darker
than coal) but very narrow,
while the inner ring is
broader but very faint. The
outermost ring has three
strange 'clumps' of material
spread along it, which
astronomers probably
mistook for ring-arcs.

Pluto and Planet X

Pluto is a tiny, cold world. It is 2400 kilometres across: just one-tenth the size of Earth. It may be an escaped moon of Neptune.

Uranus and Neptune do not orbit the Sun quite as expected and the cause was suspected to be a ninth planet. It was discovered by American astronomer Clyde Tombaugh in February 1930. While photographing the constellation Gemini, he noticed that a small object had moved position *(arrow)*; it had to be a planet. It was named Pluto after the Greek king of the underworld.

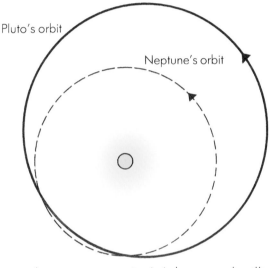

Pluto's orbit

Neptune's orbit

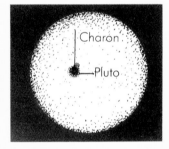

Pluto's moon Charon is 1190 kilometres in diameter; so large that they could be called a 'double planet.' Charon takes 6.4 days to orbit Pluto once.

Charon

Pluto

At its most distant point Pluto is over 7.3 thousand million kilometres from the Sun, but at its closest it is 4.4 thousand million kilometres away. Thus for a short period it is actually *inside* the orbit of Neptune.

Pluto's surface is probably ma from frozen methane. The landscape is hidden beneath atmospheric haze, but would be dominated by eerie ice structures. The Sun would bright star in the black s

THE SEARCH FOR PLANET X

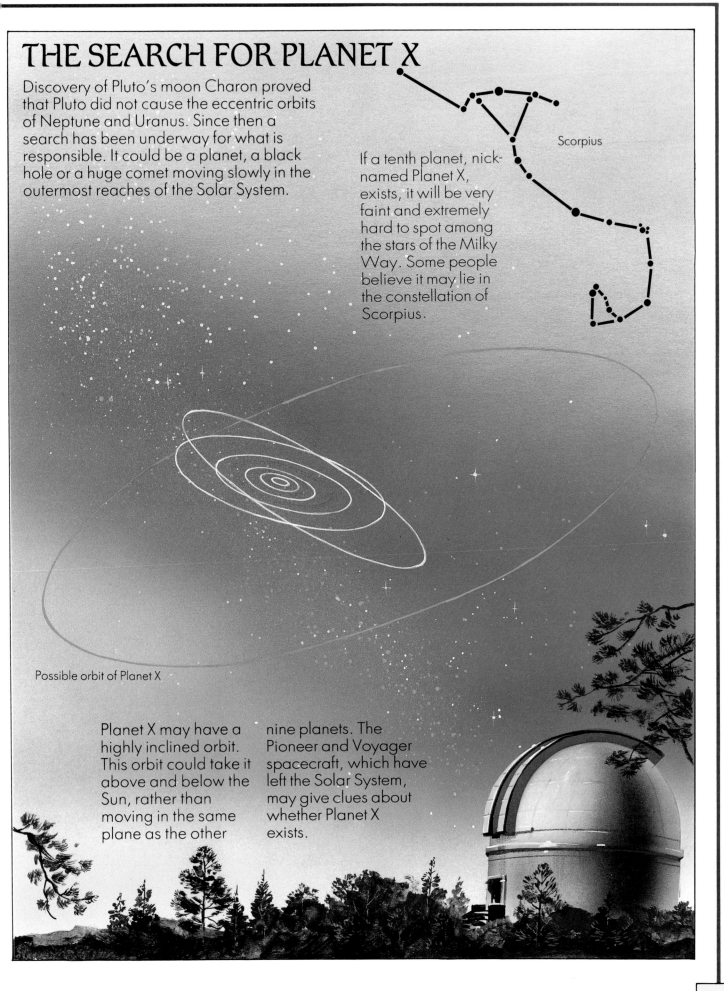

Discovery of Pluto's moon Charon proved that Pluto did not cause the eccentric orbits of Neptune and Uranus. Since then a search has been underway for what is responsible. It could be a planet, a black hole or a huge comet moving slowly in the outermost reaches of the Solar System.

If a tenth planet, nick-named Planet X, exists, it will be very faint and extremely hard to spot among the stars of the Milky Way. Some people believe it may lie in the constellation of Scorpius.

Scorpius

Possible orbit of Planet X

Planet X may have a highly inclined orbit. This orbit could take it above and below the Sun, rather than moving in the same plane as the other nine planets. The Pioneer and Voyager spacecraft, which have left the Solar System, may give clues about whether Planet X exists.

The Stars

Stars, like our Sun, are huge, luminous balls of gas fuelled by nuclear fusion. Some are bigger than the Sun, some are smaller. They are of different colours and temperatures.

Capella

Capella belongs to the same class as the Sun (Class G), but is larger and 150 times more luminous.

Betelgeuse lies in Orion and is very bright. It is a vivid red M2 star or a red supergiant and swells and shrinks like the human heart. Rigel near Betelgeuse is a brilliant blue-white class B8 star, roughly 50 times bigger than the Sun.

Betelgeuse

Sun

The Sun is a Class G star.

Arcturus is a type K2 star and is orange. It is one of the brightest stars in the sky.

Vega

Vega is a blue colour and 55 times brighter than the Sun. It is in Lyra (the Lyre) and is a Class A star.

Arcturus

Sirius, the 'Dog Star', is the brightest star in the night sky. It is 23 times more luminous than the Sun.

Sirius

VV Cephei is a huge variable star and is bluish-white.

VV Cephei

Aldebaran
Aldebaran is a red giant with a diameter of 48 million kilometres, 90 times more luminous than the Sun.

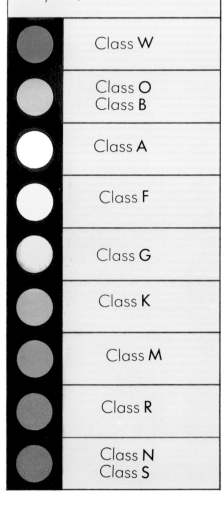

CLASSES

A very hot star will shine blue and a cooler one yellow, like the flames of a blow torch or candle. Stars are put into categories depending on how hot they are, as shown below.

	Class **W**
	Class **O** Class **B**
	Class **A**
	Class **F**
	Class **G**
	Class **K**
	Class **M**
	Class **R**
	Class **N** Class **S**

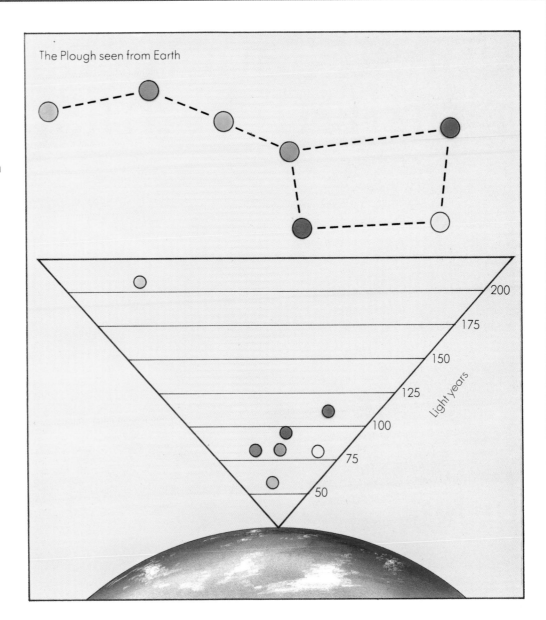

The Plough seen from Earth

The distances between the stars are so vast that they are measured in light years (the distance that light can travel in one year i.e. 9.46 million million kilometres). Proxima Centauri, the nearest star to the Sun, is 4.2 light years away.

The stars in the sky are arranged in constellations. All the stars making up a constellation, such as the Plough, seem to be the same distance away, but in fact they are scattered about in space. The diagram on the right shows the relative distances from the Earth of the stars in the Plough.

MAGNITUDE

Some stars look brighter than others simply because they are nearer the Earth. For example, viewed from Earth star B (below) seems brighter than star A, but it is really much fainter. To avoid this problem stars are given an *absolute magnitude*, i.e. how bright they would be if they were all 32.6 light years away.

From Earth star B looks brighter than A because it is nearer. It is in fact smaller and less luminous.

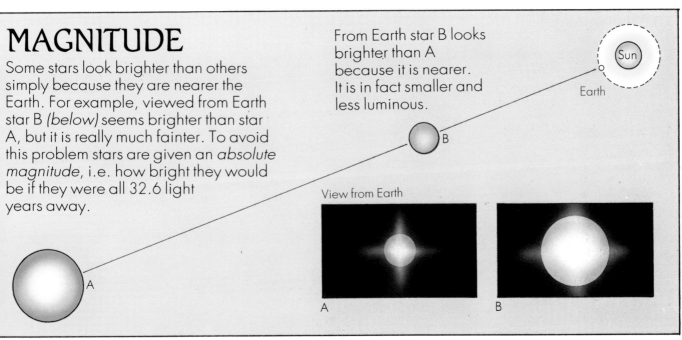

View from Earth

A   B

Constellations of the Northern Hemisphere

The starry sphere of the night sky forms two distinct halves or 'celestial hemispheres', divided by the celestial equator. Each celestial hemisphere has interesting features, such as nebulae, star clusters and constellations, which have been catalogued and mapped over many hundreds of years.

Ursa Major, The Great Bear, is one of the best known of the 88 constellations, and contains the most famous – the Plough or Big Dipper, which looks like a large spoon or ladle. The Plough is part of the Ursa Major constellation; its curved handle forms the bear's tail.

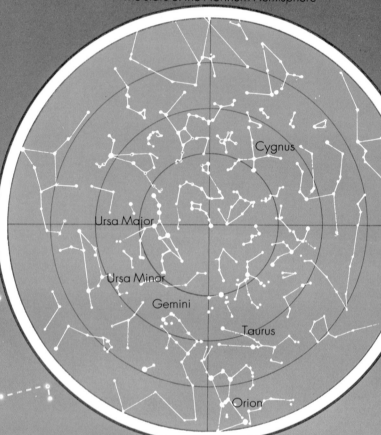

The stars of the Northern Hemisphere

Cygnus

Ursa Major

Ursa Minor

Gemini

Taurus

Orion

Ursa Major

The stars of the northern hemisphere, with Polaris, the pole star at the centre.

NOTE: these constellations are not shown in their actual positions in the night sky.

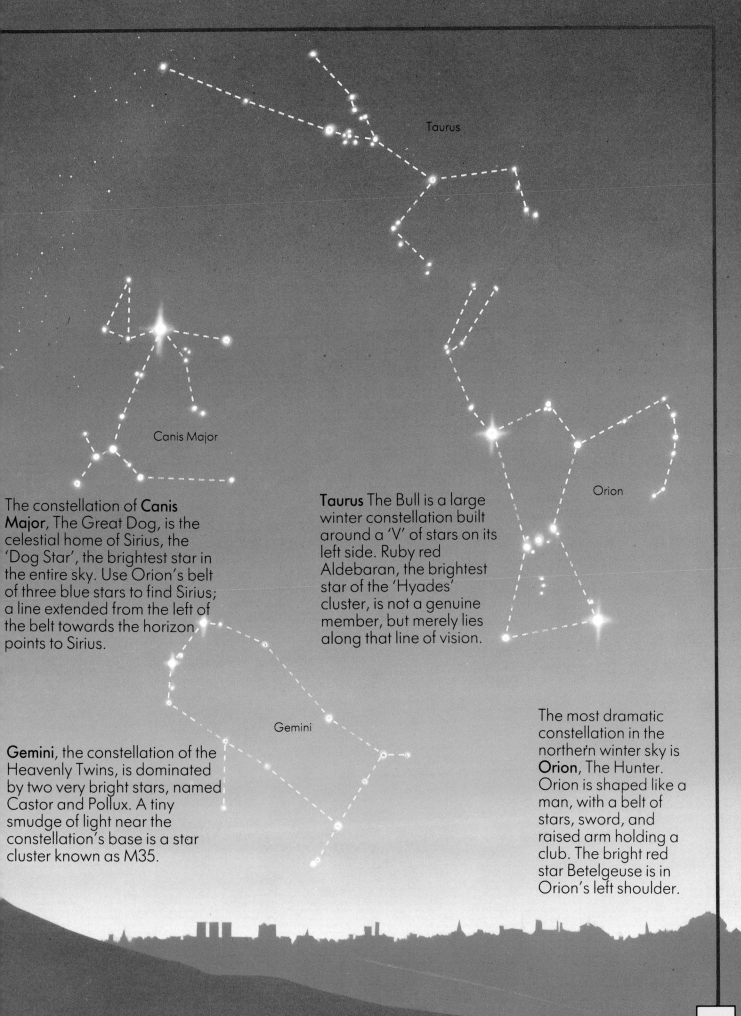

Taurus

Canis Major

Orion

Gemini

The constellation of **Canis Major**, The Great Dog, is the celestial home of Sirius, the 'Dog Star', the brightest star in the entire sky. Use Orion's belt of three blue stars to find Sirius; a line extended from the left of the belt towards the horizon points to Sirius.

Taurus The Bull is a large winter constellation built around a 'V' of stars on its left side. Ruby red Aldebaran, the brightest star of the 'Hyades' cluster, is not a genuine member, but merely lies along that line of vision.

Gemini, the constellation of the Heavenly Twins, is dominated by two very bright stars, named Castor and Pollux. A tiny smudge of light near the constellation's base is a star cluster known as M35.

The most dramatic constellation in the northern winter sky is **Orion**, The Hunter. Orion is shaped like a man, with a belt of stars, sword, and raised arm holding a club. The bright red star Betelgeuse is in Orion's left shoulder.

Constellations of the Southern Hemisphere

This is a map of the southern celestial hemisphere. It shows all the major constellations and their brighter stars, and will help you to identify them on a clear night. Obviously it cannot show the positions of the Moon or planets as they change from week to week.

The stars of the Southern Hemisphere

Centaurus

Scorpio

Southern Cross

Vela

Puppis

Sagittarius

Centaurus

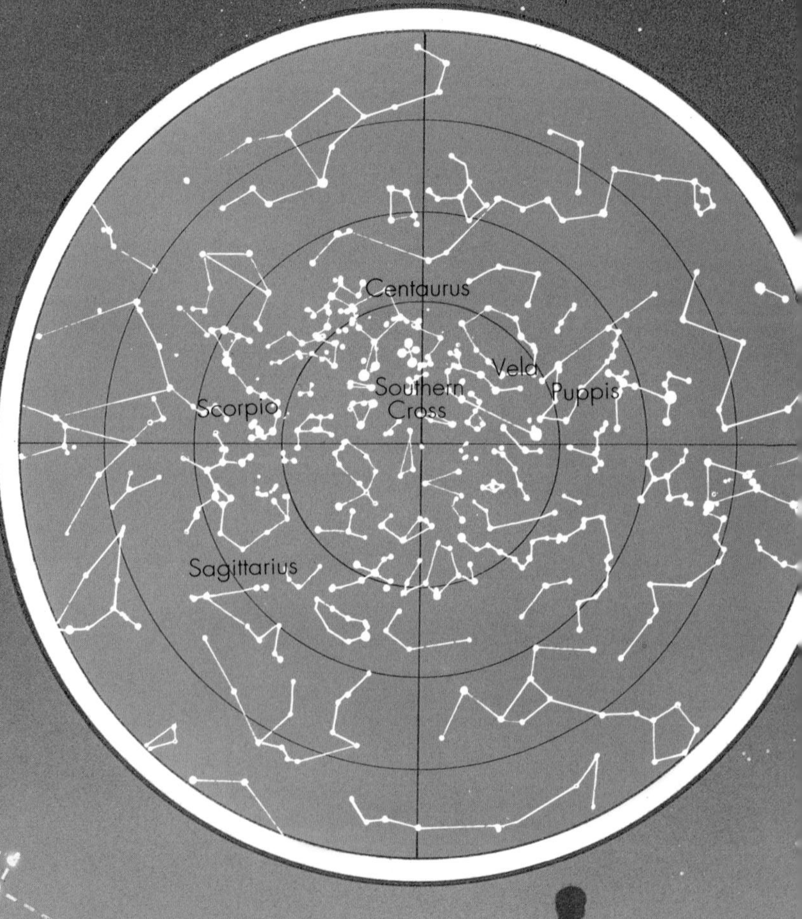

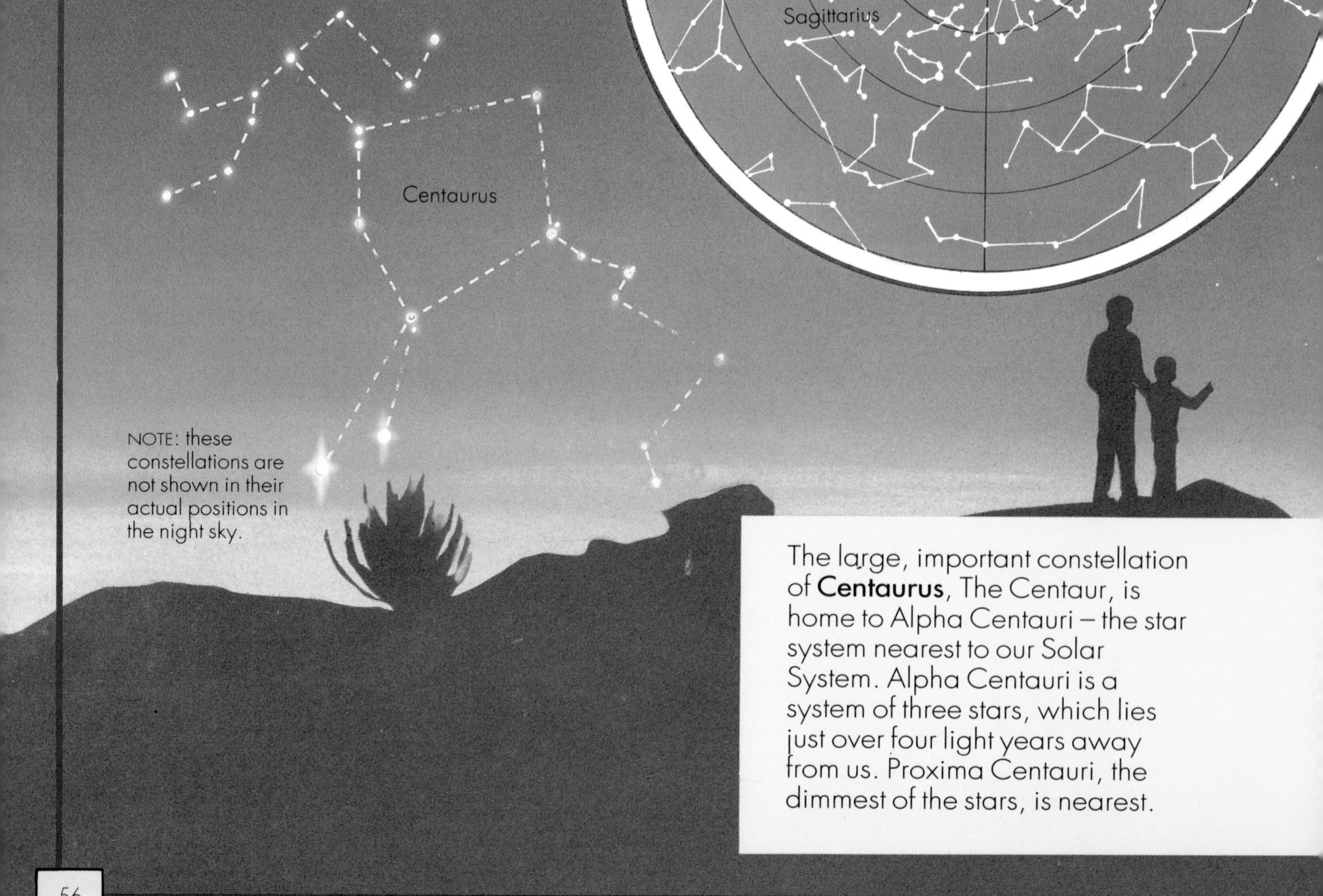

NOTE: these constellations are not shown in their actual positions in the night sky.

The large, important constellation of **Centaurus**, The Centaur, is home to Alpha Centauri – the star system nearest to our Solar System. Alpha Centauri is a system of three stars, which lies just over four light years away from us. Proxima Centauri, the dimmest of the stars, is nearest.

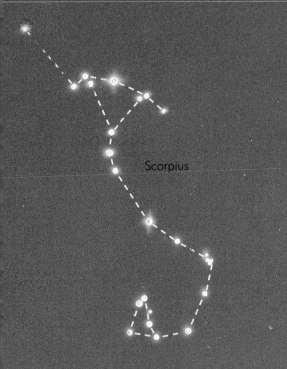

Scorpius

Sagittarius

Magellanic Cloud

uthern Cross

Sagittarius, The Archer, is a medium-sized constellation, shaped rather like an upside down teapot. It lies between us and the core of the Milky Way, apparently embedded in a mass of condensed, glittering star clouds. The brightest stars seem sometimes to vanish in the Milky Way's veil of stars.

The *Small* and *Large* **Magellanic Clouds** (named after the explorer Magellan) are two irregularly shaped galaxies which are satellites of the Milky Way. They are visible to the naked eye as misty clouds of light. The Large Cloud contains the Tarantula Nebula, a cloud of glowing crimson gas, and a supernova which exploded into view in 1987

The **Milky Way** is best seen from the southern hemisphere, from places such as Australia and South America.

The **Southern Cross** is easily identified, despite its small size and location in the star clouds of the Milky Way. On one side appears to be a dark 'hole' in the star fabric of the Milky Way; this is the *Coalsack Nebula*, a vast dark cloud silhouetted against the distant Milky Way

Lying to Sagittarius' right is **Scorpius**, the Scorpion, a curved trail of stars, resembling a fish-hook. The constellation is dominated by Antares, a red giant which shines in its head or claws. The trail of stars represents the scorpion's body and wickedly curved tail.

How Stars are Born and Die

Orion Nebula

Matter condenses into protostar

Young stars are

The Sun was born five billion years ago. The process of its birth and death is shown here.

A cloud of gas and dust is hit by the shock waves of a distant supernova and begins to condense. As the mass increases, more material is drawn inwards and the whole object begins to spin. The material in its centre starts to generate heat. When the temperature reaches 10 million °C, nuclear fusion (the making of helium from two hydrogen atoms) begins and the young star is born.

Eventually the Sun will run out of hydrogen and will begin to consume its supply of helium. Using helium as a fuel will cause the Sun to swell like an inflating balloon. When the Sun becomes a red giant, it will swallow Mercury and Venus. Heat from the Sun will scorch the Earth's surface.

Finally the star dies

Stars are constantly both being created and dying, but not all suffer the same fate. Stars bigger than the Sun live accelerated lives. Because they are so big, these stars need huge quantities of hydrogen to fuel their nuclear reactions, and so run out of hydrogen very quickly. They eventually blow apart in a huge supernova explosion. Stars smaller than the Sun never become hot enough to cause a supernova explosion, and slowly fade away.

It cools further

Eventually the star becomes a white dwarf

The star condenses further

The centre of the sta shrinks and blows o atmosphere, formin planetary nebula

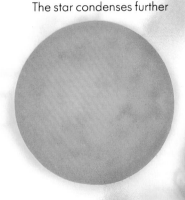

Young sun grows

Sun as it is today

Six billion years from now the Earth will have been destroyed. After a few million years as a red giant, the Sun will begin to shrink. The outer layers will be blown away to try and maintain its delicate balance, forming a halo called a planetary nebula. The Sun will continue to shrink until it is a white dwarf. It will continue to shine, but will gradually cool until the last heat radiates away.

After 10 billion years the star runs out of hydrogen and swells

Sun burns helium and swells further

The star becomes a huge red giant – 100 times bigger than our Sun is today.

Supernovae

Star exhausts energy supply

Core contracts, then explodes

Temperatures can reach 5000 million°C

A supernova is the result of the violent death of a massive star. In the first ten seconds of the explosion, it produces 100 times more energy than the Sun during the whole of its 10 billion year lifetime …!

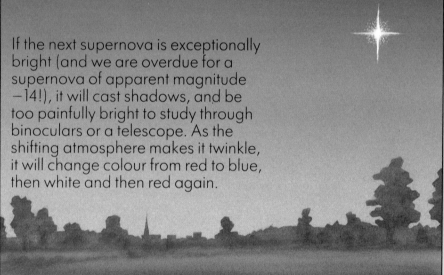

If the next supernova is exceptionally bright (and we are overdue for a supernova of apparent magnitude −14!), it will cast shadows, and be too painfully bright to study through binoculars or a telescope. As the shifting atmosphere makes it twinkle, it will change colour from red to blue, then white and then red again.

After exhausting its supply of hydrogen the star's interior contracts, and its temperature soars. This increase in core temperature ignites a new and heavier fuel – the gas helium. However, the helium is soon used up and carbon is used a replacement fuel. The core contracts and the increase in temperature ignites even heavier elements, until eventually only a dense core of iron remains, surrounded by layers of silicon, oxygen, carbon, helium and hydrogen. The iron core absorbs rather than giving out energy. With the energy source gone, the star collapses and the force given out causes the supernova to explode, reaching a temperature of perhaps 5 thousand million°C. The remaining core becomes a pulsar, a spinning neutron star emitting pulses of light and radio waves.

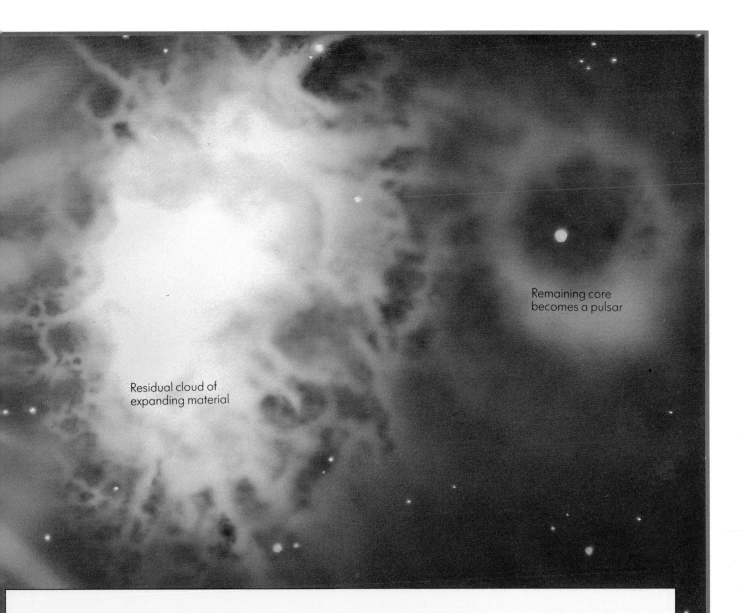

Remaining core
becomes a pulsar

Residual cloud of
expanding material

TYCHO'S STAR

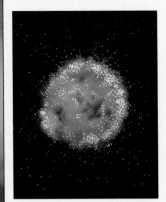

On 11 November
1572, the Danish
astronomer Tycho
Brahe saw a new
star in Cassiopeia.

CRAB NEBULA

The crab nebula
(*above*) is the remains
of a supernova which
appeared over China
in 1054.

SUPERNOVA 1987A

The brightest supernova for 383 years
appeared in February 1987 in the
Magellanic cloud in the Southern
Hemisphere. It represented the death of a
blue giant 20 times bigger than the Sun and
80,000 times as bright.

Black Holes and Strange Stars

Gas and material lying close to the black hole are attracted to it like water going down a plug hole. Some astronomers think that the more a black hole 'eats', the bigger it becomes. If this is true, there may be Super Black Holes 'eating' the equivalent of three Earths every second – or 95 million every year.

If we could travel into space to a black hole, what would it look like? In a region of empty space, it would literally appear as a hole in space. If it was near a cloud of interstellar gas, material drawn towards the star would spiral around it into a disc. It would shine with different types of radiation, giving the dark, central core a glowing halo of light.

Black hole

A black hole is not a 'hole', but a solid, spherical object formed after the death of a massive star. After the star has died all that remains is a tiny, super-dense star several kilometres wide. Its gravitational pull is so strong that not even light can escape it; so it appears as a black hole cut into the background stars.

Nearby star

In 1962 a rocket detected strong X-ray radiation in the constellation of Cygnus. Five years later, astronomers located the source as what they thought could be a black hole – possibly the remnant of an ancient supernova explosion. If this is correct, then material is drawn away from nearby stars in a glowing stream, then coiled around the black hole before it is sucked to oblivion.

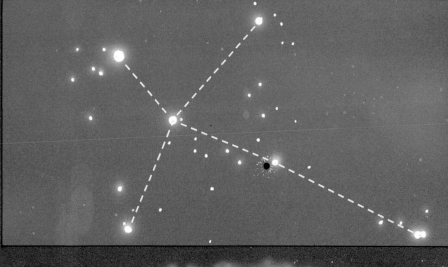

Some astronomers believe that a massive black hole may lie at the centre of the Milky Way. Using special instruments they have detected a strong radiation source 1.5 billion kilometres in diameter (roughly the distance between the Earth and Saturn). At the very centre of this source might lie a black hole 15 million kilometres wide.

RED GIANT

When a star the size of our Sun has consumed all its fuel, it briefly swells into a huge red giant, before shrinking to become a white dwarf roughly the size of Earth. A white dwarf is a super dense object, from which a handful of matter would weigh thousands of tons! There are several. The brightest star in the sky, Sirius, has a tiny white dwarf companion, Sirius B, just 19,000 kilometres wide.

White dwarf

Sun

Red giant

NEUTRON STAR

A neutron star is the core of a star three or more times more massive than the Sun which has been in a supernova explosion. One pinhead of its strange material would weigh more than one million tonnes – more than the biggest aircraft carrier in the world! Many neutron stars are *pulsars*. Pulsars are rapidly spinning stars that send out beams of radiation that sweep across space.

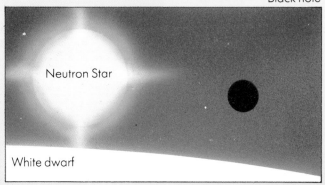

Black hole

Neutron Star

White dwarf

Galaxies

Galaxies are vast collections of stars, gas and dust, held together in one of several different shapes by gravity. They are the 'building blocks' of the Universe. The Milky Way is just one of millions of galaxies drifting through space, and astronomers often call the Milky Way our 'island' in the ocean of space. Although our home galaxy is massive when compared to our solar system, it is just one tiny part of the Universe.

Spiral galaxy

Barred spiral galaxies are very similar to Spiral galaxies, but their spiral arms curve away from the opposite ends of a bar, passing through the centre of the nucleus. They contain large amounts of gas and dust as well as stars.

Barred spiral galaxy

Spiral galaxies are shaped like catherine wheels, with several spiral arms curving away from their centre. Some spiral arms are wound much more tightly than others, and contain not only stars, but also dark trailing lanes of dust and clouds of glowing gas. At their centre is a bulging nucleus of old red stars, possibly surrounding a massive black hole. The Milky Way is a typical spiral galaxy.

Elliptical galaxies are huge collections of stars with an elliptical or egg-like shape. They consist almost entirely of stars and contain very little gas or dust.

Irregular galaxies are, as their name suggests, irregular collections of stars without any definite shape.

Elliptical galaxy

Irregular galaxy

FORMATION OF THE GALAXIES

Typical spiral galaxies began when a massive dust and gas cloud began to collapse in on itself into a roughly spherical shape. Condensations formed and became star clusters. The denser, central portions of the sphere flattened out into a revolving disc. After about a billion years, spiral arms began to form out of the disc, containing dense lumps of material which contracted further to form clusters of stars. They soon exploded, spewing rich stellar material through the young galaxy to recondense into smaller stars.

The Milky Way

The Milky Way is just one of 100 billion galaxies in the Universe. It contains over 100 billion stars.

The Milky Way is a massive pin-wheel of over 100 billion stars. Our sun is just one of these.

Just like a giant catherine wheel, our galaxy rotates. To make one complete revolution takes 230 million years — since it was formed, our galaxy has revolved 52 times.

The nucleus of our galaxy is made up of ancient red giant stars. Some astronomers think a giant black hole may lie in the centre.

The milky way from earth

From Earth we can see the Milky Way as a broad band of misty light, at its brightest during summer.

We are here

As well as rotating, the Milky Way is actually moving through space at a speed of 2.2 million kilometres per hour...

Seen from the side, the Milky Way resembles a discus. Our solar system lies two-thirds of the way from the centre.

The Solar System

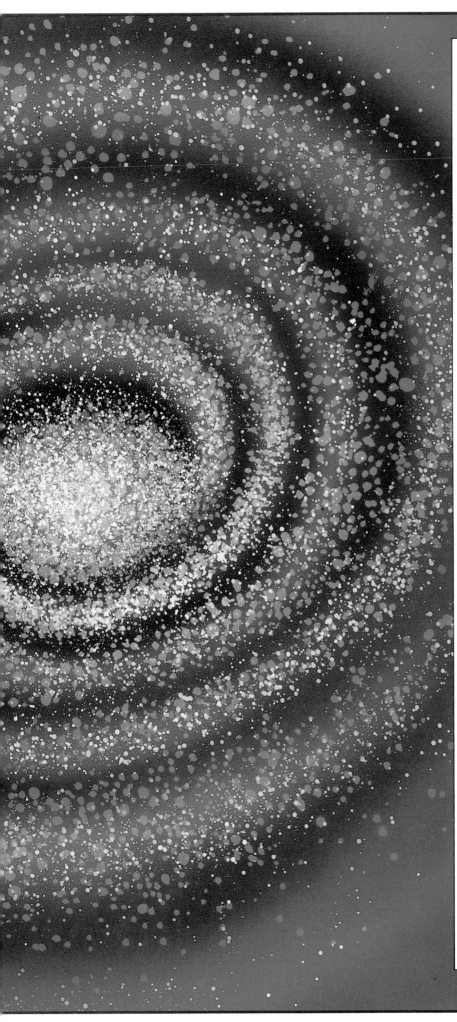

Star Clusters

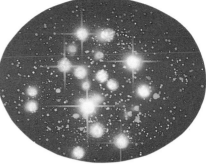

There are many star clusters in our galaxy. Open clusters (*above*) contain hundreds of stars whilst denser globular clusters contain millions of stars.

Nebulae (*above*) are clouds of gas which lie between the stars. They can be either dark or, if they reflect the light of nearby stars, bright.

The Milky Way is constantly producing new stars, one is born approximately every eighteen days!

Comets

Comets are thought to come from the 'Oort Cloud', a halo of over 100 billion comets surrounding our Solar System far beyond the orbit of Pluto.

People used to think comets were fireballs, but the exact opposite is true. They are frozen, lifeless bodies most of the time and wake up only when they near the Sun.

A comet's nucleus is like an iceberg. As it nears the Sun, the ice melts, releasing the gas trapped inside.

Some comets pass so close to the Sun that astronomers call them 'sun-grazers'. In 1965 Comet Ikeya Seki passed just 464,000 kilometres above the Sun's surface – just slightly farther than the Moon is from the Earth.

A comet's tail always points away from the Sun. The gases released from the nucleus get blown behind it by the solar wind.

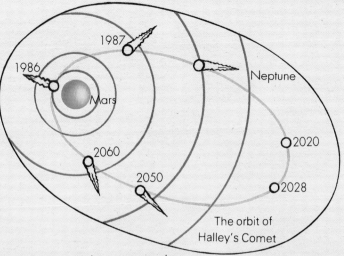

1987

1986

Neptune

Mars

2060

2050

2020

2028

The orbit of Halley's Comet

The Great Comet of 1843 had the longest recorded tail, stretching over 800 million kilometres – roughly the same distance as the Earth is from Jupiter.

A comet has two tails. The dust tail is yellow because it reflects sunlight, and the gas tail is blue as it shines with its own light.

Most comets appear to have only one tail, as the gas tail is very faint. However, some comets have several tails. Comet de Cheseaux had six.

HALLEY'S COMET

Halley's comet was named after Edmund Halley, the scientist who worked out that comets have orbits. It can be traced far back in history – William the Conqueror saw it in 1066. It was last seen in 1986 and will return in 2062.

In 1986 the space probe Giotto took close-up photographs of Halley's comet. Seconds later it was knocked off course by a blast of dust.

Meteors and meteorites

Shooting stars which astronomers term 'meteors', are not really stars, but much smaller objects. They range in size from a grain of rice to several centimetres. A meteor plunges into our atmosphere, and becomes very hot because of the air molecules rubbing against it. For a split second it is visible, glowing like a star and shooting across the sky. The dust soon burns to a cinder, and vanishes. Meteors are pieces of material left over from the birth of the Solar System five thousand million years ago.

Saturn

Meteoroid Stream

Sun

Earth

Mars

Jupiter

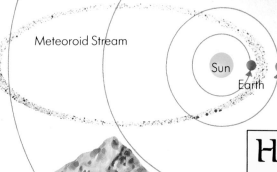

Most shooting stars burn up completely, but one large enough may fall to Earth as a charred piece of rock, or meteorite.

HUNTING METEORITES

Meteorites are difficult to find because they are small and easily lost on the ground. However, Antarctica is excellent for meteorite-hunting, as the charred stones stand out clearly against the snow and ice. Often they are just lying on the surface.

Some meteors are coloured, most often blue and white, though some may be red, or even green.

In 1966 a magnificent display of shooting stars occurred, and for a brief period over 1000 meteors were flashing across the sky every second! Some observers said the shooting stars were 'falling like snow'

On any clear night you can expect to see at least one bright shooting star. Some are barely visible, others bright enough to cast shadows. Most are as bright as an average star, and easy to spot.

The best known crater on Earth is the huge 'Meteor Crater' in Arizona, USA. It is 1.2 kilometres wide, more than 183 metres deep, and only properly visible from the air. It was formed 50,000 years ago, when a large meteorite 30 metres wide struck the Earth.

Space Travel Origins

Alan Shepard, in a Mercury capsule, was the first American into space, but he never reached orbit.

During World War 2 German scientists built a rocket to attack London from the continent. Each V2 rocket was 14 metres high, had a range of 320 kilometres and carried 5000 kilograms of explosives. After the war the V2 scientists helped America to develop a space rocket.

V2 rocket

By AD 970 the Chinese had designed a bamboo tube filled with gunpowder on the tip of a long arrow. When fired, this 'rocket-arrow' would travel a long distance over battlefields before exploding.

The world's first ever artificial satellite, Sputnik 1, was launched on the 4th of October 1957 by the Soviet Union. Tiny compared to today's massive communications satellites, Sputnik 1 was really a polished metal sphere the size of a beach-ball with a radio transmitter inside.

Sputnik rocket

In April 1961, Major Yuri Gagarin became the first man into space. He travelled around the Earth in Vostok 1, a modified unmanned satellite, for 1 hour and 18 minutes, and returned to Earth 108 minutes after leaving the launch pad.

Vostok 1 and Yuri Gagarin

Sputnik 1

Vostok rocket

Laika, first animal in spac

The first live creature to in space was a fox terri called Laika. She was carried aboard Sputnik on 3 November 1957, and spent a week in or There was no way to bring her back to Earth alive, and she died in h sleep when the capsule oxygen ran out.

Gemini 7

The US Skylab space station was an American triumph. The 'workshop' of the station was actually a converted rocket stage which contained experiments, work stations, food stores and living quarters. Skylab crews travelled to the space station in modified Apollo spacecraft, and docked into a cylindrical Docking Adapter. Power for Skylab was provided by solar cells mounted on two large wing-like panels, only one of which actually opened.

Skylab

The Gemini programme, costing $1 billion, linked spacecraft in oribit as a first step in sending astronauts to the Moon.

The Space Shuttles

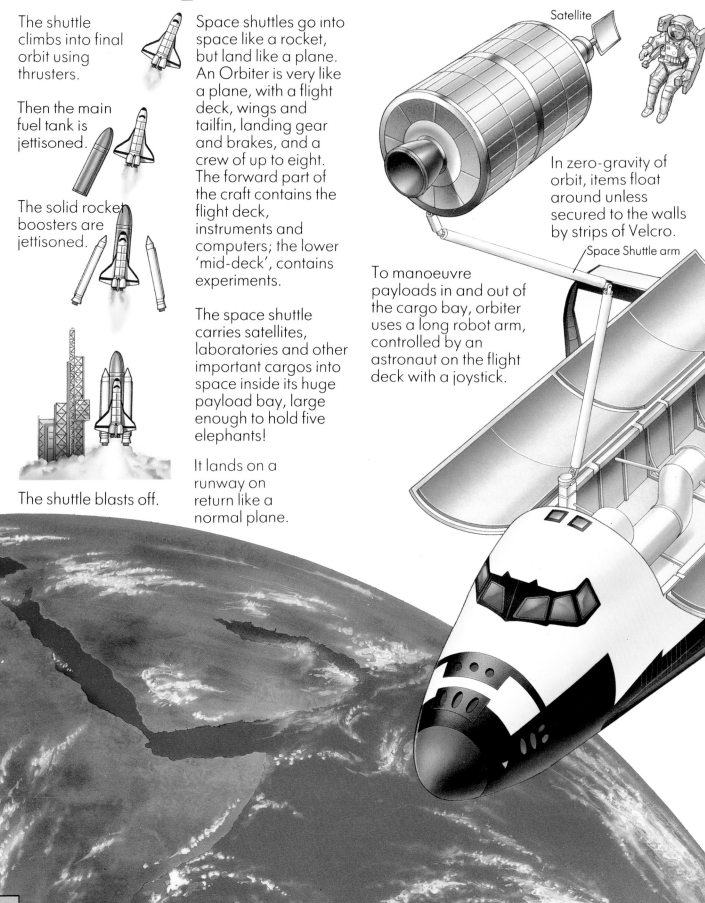

The shuttle climbs into final orbit using thrusters.

Then the main fuel tank is jettisoned.

The solid rocket boosters are jettisoned.

The shuttle blasts off.

Space shuttles go into space like a rocket, but land like a plane. An Orbiter is very like a plane, with a flight deck, wings and tailfin, landing gear and brakes, and a crew of up to eight. The forward part of the craft contains the flight deck, instruments and computers; the lower 'mid-deck', contains experiments.

The space shuttle carries satellites, laboratories and other important cargos into space inside its huge payload bay, large enough to hold five elephants!

It lands on a runway on return like a normal plane.

Satellite

In zero-gravity of orbit, items float around unless secured to the walls by strips of Velcro.

Space Shuttle arm

To manoeuvre payloads in and out of the cargo bay, orbiter uses a long robot arm, controlled by an astronaut on the flight deck with a joystick.

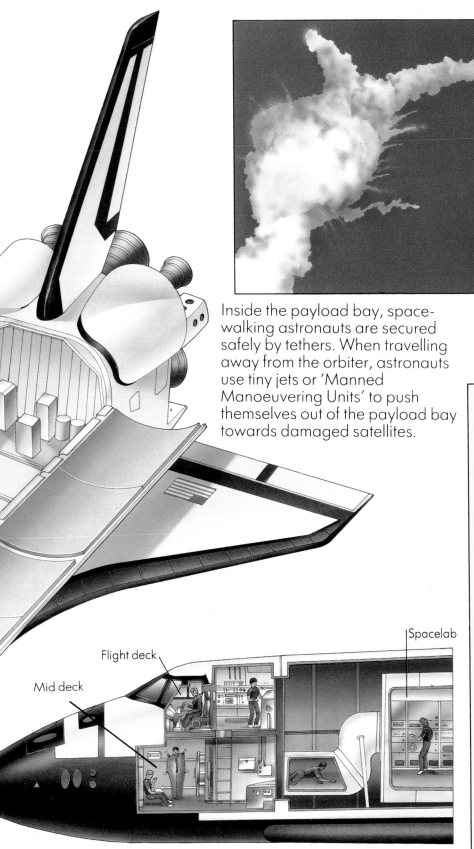

In 1986 the space shuttle Challenger blasted off from the launch pad for the 25th shuttle mission. On board were six American astronauts and a school-teacher, Christa McAuliffe, the first civilian to fly in space. 73 seconds after blast-off, the shuttle exploded in a fireball, and all the astronauts were killed (*left*). The disaster happened because one of the solid rocket boosters was faulty.

Inside the payload bay, space-walking astronauts are secured safely by tethers. When travelling away from the orbiter, astronauts use tiny jets or 'Manned Manoeuvering Units' to push themselves out of the payload bay towards damaged satellites.

Flight deck

Mid deck

Spacelab

THE SOVIET SHUTTLE

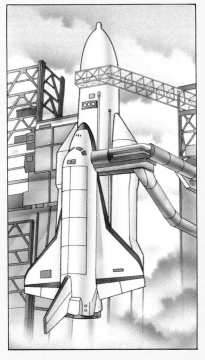

The first Soviet Space Shuttle, *Buran*, was unmanned. It was almost exactly like the US Shuttle, but it had no main engines and reached orbit on the side of the *Energiya* rocket.

After a hard day's work the crew retire to their beds. Two of the beds are like chests of drawers, with doors which slide shut; the third bed is vertical, like a shower cubicle. All the beds have sleeping bags instead of mattresses, and straps secure astronauts' arms and legs to prevent them from drifting around in the weightless conditions.

Satellites

A communications satellite bounces signals sent from one point on the Earth back down to another point. Among the most important comsats are the Intelsats, which transfer international telephone calls. **Intelsat 5**, the latest satellite in the Intelsat network, run by 100 countries, can carry up to 33,000 simultaneous telephone conversations.

From their orbits, 'Earth Resource' satellites such as **Landsat** take thousands of pictures of the Earth's surface, mapping areas of vegetation and mineral deposits. As well as surface geology, the satellite searches underground, to locate water under the desert and potential areas for oil exploration under the ocean. The satellites can also take high resolution photographs of towns and cities.

Meteosat, a weather satellite, orbits in a geostationary orbit, appearing to hover 36,000 kilometres above the equator. It can take several different types of pictures at once. One camera photographs visible light features like clouds.

Landsat

Intelsat

The KH-11 spy satellites – nicknamed 'Key-Hole' – can stay in orbit for over two years. More than 18 metres tall and weighing 13,000 kilograms, their highly sensitive sensors can zoom in on individual soldiers hundreds of kilometres below!

Another camera take infra-red shots of different temperature areas. Another camera might measure narrow infra red wavelengths. The also record areas of atmospheric humidity

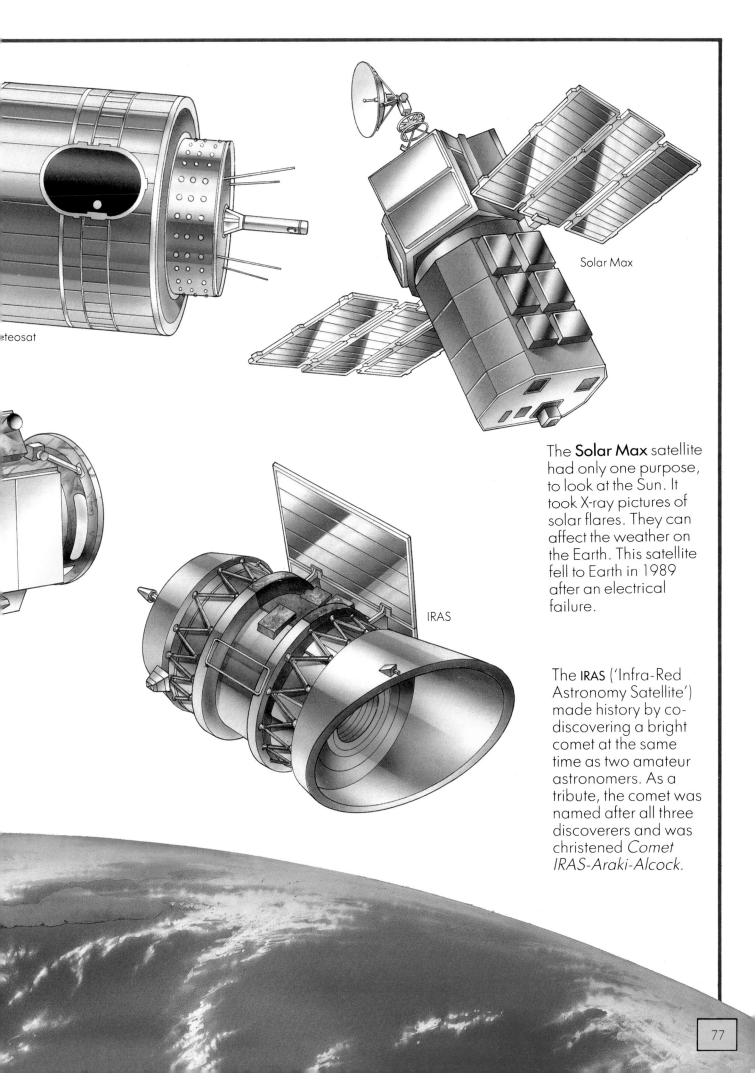

teosat

Solar Max

IRAS

The **Solar Max** satellite had only one purpose, to look at the Sun. It took X-ray pictures of solar flares. They can affect the weather on the Earth. This satellite fell to Earth in 1989 after an electrical failure.

The IRAS ('Infra-Red Astronomy Satellite') made history by co-discovering a bright comet at the same time as two amateur astronomers. As a tribute, the comet was named after all three discoverers and was christened *Comet IRAS-Araki-Alcock.*

Space Probes Explore the Solar System

During the past 30 years space probes have visited all the planets in the Solar System except Pluto. Mariner 10 (1) reached Mercury in March 1974, taking over 8000 photographs of the barren, cratered landscape. It is now in permanent orbit around the Sun. The Pioneer Venus orbiter (4) travelled 500 kilometres, reached Venus in December 1978 and sent back radar maps of the Venusian surface. Viking probes (3) landed on the surface of Mars in 1976 by parachute, tested the soil for signs of life and found none. In 1992 the Mars Observer space probe was launched, to map the Red Planet in more detail than ever before. Voyagers 1 and 2 explored the outer planets. Voyager 2 (2) sent back stunning pictures of Neptune in 1989. Magellan (5) reached Venus in 1990.

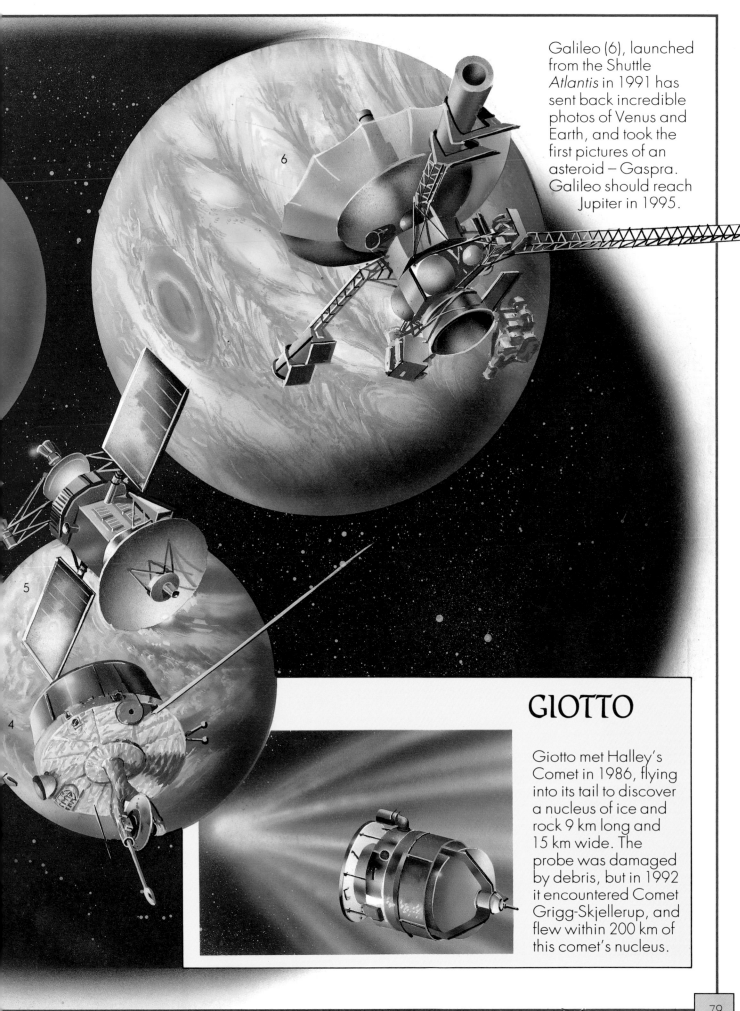

Galileo (6), launched from the Shuttle *Atlantis* in 1991 has sent back incredible photos of Venus and Earth, and took the first pictures of an asteroid – Gaspra. Galileo should reach Jupiter in 1995.

GIOTTO

Giotto met Halley's Comet in 1986, flying into its tail to discover a nucleus of ice and rock 9 km long and 15 km wide. The probe was damaged by debris, but in 1992 it encountered Comet Grigg-Skjellerup, and flew within 200 km of this comet's nucleus.

Voyager

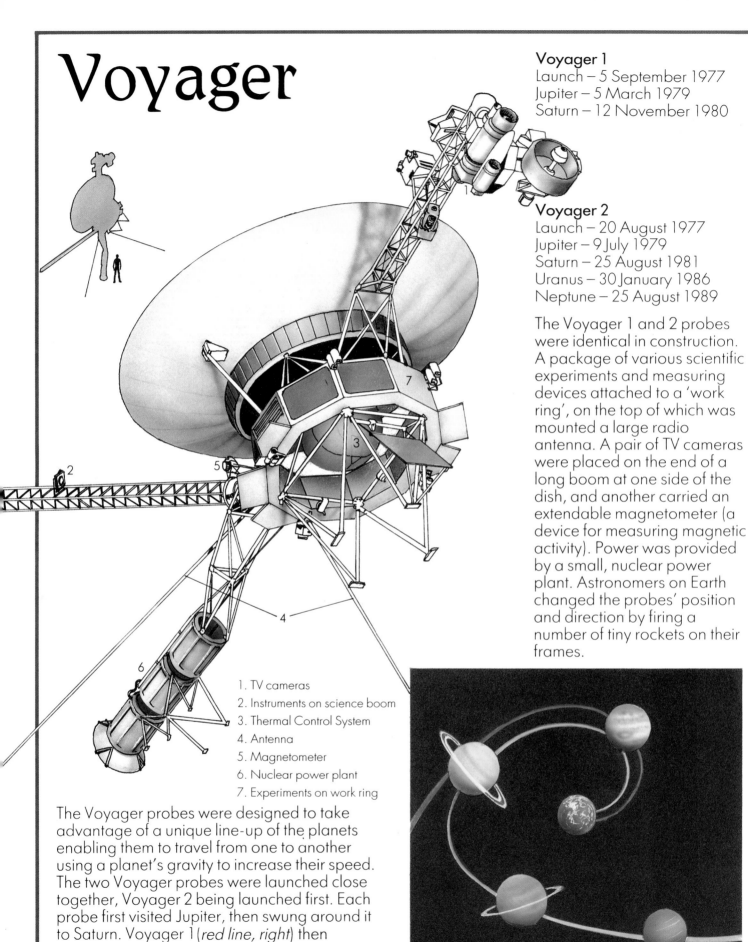

Voyager 2
Launch – 20 August 1977
Jupiter – 9 July 1979
Saturn – 25 August 1981
Uranus – 30 January 1986
Neptune – 25 August 1989

The Voyager 1 and 2 probes were identical in construction. A package of various scientific experiments and measuring devices attached to a 'work ring', on the top of which was mounted a large radio antenna. A pair of TV cameras were placed on the end of a long boom at one side of the dish, and another carried an extendable magnetometer (a device for measuring magnetic activity). Power was provided by a small, nuclear power plant. Astronomers on Earth changed the probes' position and direction by firing a number of tiny rockets on their frames.

1. TV cameras
2. Instruments on science boom
3. Thermal Control System
4. Antenna
5. Magnetometer
6. Nuclear power plant
7. Experiments on work ring

The Voyager probes were designed to take advantage of a unique line-up of the planets enabling them to travel from one to another using a planet's gravity to increase their speed. The two Voyager probes were launched close together, Voyager 2 being launched first. Each probe first visited Jupiter, then swung around it to Saturn. Voyager 1 (*red line, right*) then headed out of the Solar system. Voyager 2 (*yellow line, right*) travelled to Uranus and Neptune before it also left the Solar System.

VOYAGERS' DISCOVERIES

Jupiter

Saturn

The Voyagers took amazing photographs of Jupiter's swirling, multi-coloured clouds.

The Voyager probes discovered Saturn's rings were made of thousands and thousands of tiny ringlets. They discovered many new small moons in orbit and took detailed pictures, of its major moons, including Mimas and Titan.

Io

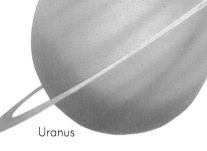

Uranus

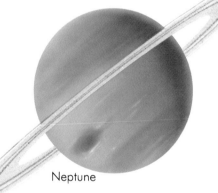

Neptune

Voyager 1 discovered active sulphur volcanoes on Jupiter's orange moon Io.

Voyager 2 revealed Uranus to be a bland, featureless world. Its tiny moon, Miranda, was revealed as the most fascinating satellite of the solar system, with towering ice cliffs and a strange, grooved surface.

Neptune was powder-blue, with a storm called the Great Dark Spot. It showed astronomers the moon Triton's surface for the first time.

A MESSAGE

In case any other being found the drifting Voyager, scientists fixed a plaque and a record onto its side. The plaque shows a man, woman and child, and a simple map to show Earth's location in space. The record contains sounds, ranging from classical music to greetings in many languages. The record could also show them 118 pictures, including a human skeleton, the ocean, a snow-topped mountain and – of course – the Earth seen from space.

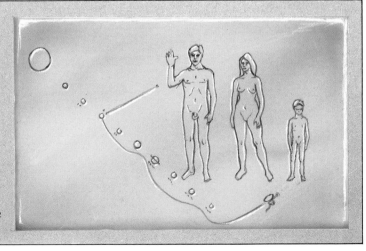

The Attempts to Reach Mars

Many different spaceprobes have visited Mars over the years. Several American Mariner probes were sent to the Red Planet in the 1960s and 1970s. They were followed by the Viking probes which analysed the soil in mini laboratories. In 1989 the twin Soviet Phobos probes both failed before reaching Martian orbit.

In 1994 Russia plans to explore Mars with several balloons. These will drift around Mars, taking photographs, and measurements such as wind speed. These balloons will be followed by Robot Rovers, which will trundle across the plains under remote control. Before a manned expedition is staged a sample of Martian soil will be taken by a robot lander and returned to Earth for analysis.

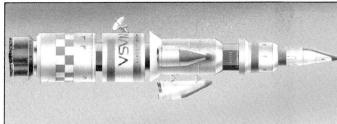

The USA hopes to send a manned mission to Mars after they have built the Alpha space station and established a base on the Moon. Astronauts may head for Mars as early as the year 2019. The Mars spaceship will be so large that it will be built in orbit, assembled from different sections carried into orbit by rockets and space shuttles. It will have powerful rocket motors and several Landers.

While the landing team explore the Martian surface, the astronauts left behind in the mothership will study Mars from orbit.

When the ship enters Martian orbit her crew will finally select the landing site by photographing the surface through high powered telescopes. Then they will check the systems of the lander craft itself.

After separating from the mothership the lander will leave orbit by firing rockets to slow it down. After flying through the atmosphere it will drop to the surface on parachutes, slowed by its braking engines.

After the astronauts from the first lander have explored their landing site, taking rock samples and setting up instruments, other landers will descend to the surface, landing nearby to create a Mars Base.

After docking with the mothership the triumphant explorers will rejoin their crewmates and prepare for the return to Earth. They will take final photographs of Mars and dump all their waste into space before shutting down all the mothership's systems and entering the return stage, carrying with them all the photographs, rock samples and data they have gathered during their stay. The crew will fire the return stage's engines and leave mars orbit for Earth, leaving the mothership behind as a Mars Orbital Space Station.

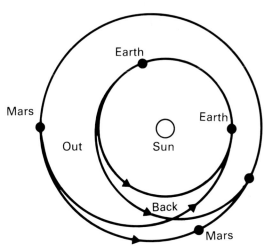

To reach Mars, the astronauts will have to spend nearly two years in space. If they set off for Mars in December 2019 they would reach their destination nine months later. After spending four months on the surface they would set a course for Earth once more, returning home in September 2021.

After securing their Base against the elements and shutting down all its power systems the astronauts will strap themselves into the upper stage of a lander. Using the descent stage as a launch pad the upper stage will blast-off and head for an orbital rendezvous with the mothership.

After the first successful manned expedition to Mars, other missions are planned to follow, increasing the size of the Martian base with additional modules and equipment. It is hoped that it will become a permanent colony, producing its own water and fuel, and also growing its own food.

Man in Space

By the year 2015 revolutionary new spacecraft called spaceplanes may be going into orbit. These vehicles will be cheaper than space shuttles. Instead of carrying huge fuel tanks of liquid oxygen they will 'breathe' oxygen from the Earth's atmosphere. They will use a normal aircraft runway, and carry dozens of passengers each time.

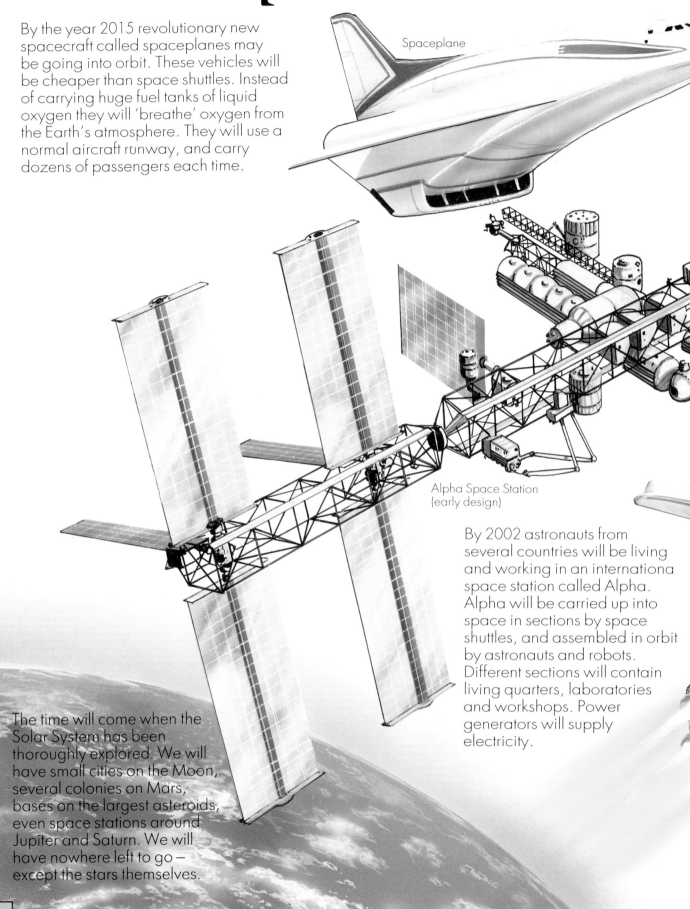

Spaceplane

Alpha Space Station
(early design)

By 2002 astronauts from several countries will be living and working in an international space station called Alpha. Alpha will be carried up into space in sections by space shuttles, and assembled in orbit by astronauts and robots. Different sections will contain living quarters, laboratories and workshops. Power generators will supply electricity.

The time will come when the Solar System has been thoroughly explored. We will have small cities on the Moon, several colonies on Mars, bases on the largest asteroids, even space stations around Jupiter and Saturn. We will have nowhere left to go — except the stars themselves.

MOONBASE

The Apollo progammes of the 1960s and 70s showed that we can work on the Moon for short periods, but a proper lunar base is needed to learn more about our nearest space neighbour. From·the base astronomers will study the sky, and doctors make new medicines.

MARS BASE

The first missions to Mars will study the surface and collect samples, but later crews will take the first sections of a Martian base. Some ten years after the first landing there could be a team of a dozen astronauts living on Mars; ten years later the number could be ten times that.

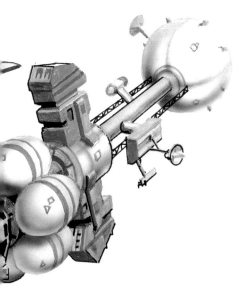

When interstellar flight finally becomes feasible, journeys will still take years rather than days or months.

ET/UFO's

UFOs – Unidentified Flying Objects – are believed by many to be the spacecraft of alien lifeforms, first reported by a pilot who saw 'flying saucer-like objects' in the late 1950s. But the most common sighting is still of a craft with a spinning dome and bumps on the sides. Some are hoaxes, but others cannot simply be explained away…

Many people who claim to have seen UFOs also claim to have seen the strange alien beings which pilot them. Some are huge and hairy, others very small like dwarves; some speak English, and others an amazing alien tongue. Some witnesses say they were taken into the aliens' spaceship for medical examinations or a space journey!

The world of science fiction has given us many aliens. Perhaps, out there in space, there really are aliens like these...

The Daleks are Dr Who's arch enemies. The protective metal casings contain jelly-like creatures called Kaleds.

E.T. – The Extra Terrestrial – was left stranded on Earth by his spaceship. He eventually returned home safely.

The alien from the film Alien was covered in spines, with razor-sharp teeth and sharp claws, and was almost indestructible.

If aliens really do exist, how they will look when we find them will depend on what sort of a planet they come from. The human shape reflects the nature of the Earth's atmosphere and environment and the strength of its gravity. Other planets have different conditions.

Lifeforms on a planet with strong gravity will be squashed towards the ground. They might have huge, leathery feet.

On a low gravity planet the aliens' bones would be able to grow and grow, possibly reaching five metres tall.

It has been suggested that if life existed on gaseous planets, it might be ray-like creatures with leathery wings.

IS THERE ANYBODY OUT THERE?

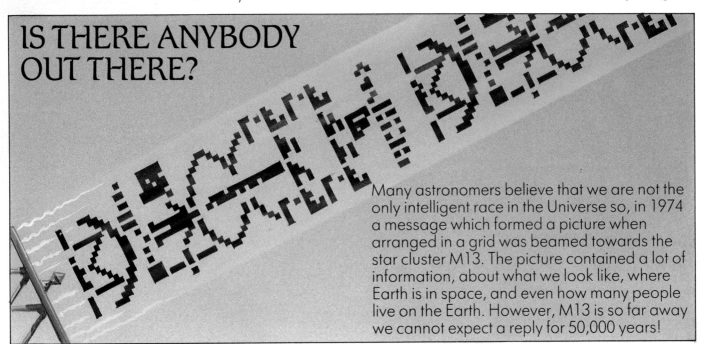

Many astronomers believe that we are not the only intelligent race in the Universe so, in 1974 a message which formed a picture when arranged in a grid was beamed towards the star cluster M13. The picture contained a lot of information, about what we look like, where Earth is in space, and even how many people live on the Earth. However, M13 is so far away we cannot expect a reply for 50,000 years!

GLOSSARY

Artificial Satellite A mechanical object launched by a rocket from earth which orbits a natural body, such as a planet or a moon etc.

Asterism An easily identifiable shape of stars in the night sky, such as a cross, a line or a circle. Always as a part of a constellation.

Asteroid A small, irregular-shaped body which orbits the Sun like a miniature planet. Most lie in a belt between Mars and Jupiter.

Astronaut A man or woman who travels beyond the Earth and into space. Russian astronauts are called *Cosmonauts*.

Astronomers Astronomers are scientists who study the heavens and all the objects in space, using telescopes and other equipment.

Astronomy The scientific study of all the objects in the heavens.

Atmosphere The blanket of different gases which surrounds and covers a planet or moon. It may be breathable or poisonous.

Aurora Borealis/ Australis Or *Northern Lights*: curtains of coloured light which shine in the night sky above the Earth's poles, (Borealis = north, Australis = south).

Big Bang Astronomers think that the Universe was formed in a massive explosion – the Big Bang – 15 billion years ago. Before then there was nothing.

Black Hole A object with such a strong gravitational pull that not even light rays can escape it. So this theoretical object appears completely black.

Colony A permanently manned base which in the future may be built on Mars and the Moon. These bases will need to be big enough to grow crops and feed all the inhabitants without returning to Earth.

Comet A comet has a solid nucleus of dirty ice, a gaseous coma, and two tails made out of gas released by the heat of the sun as the comet passes by.

Comet Nucleus The solid heart of a comet – a dirty iceberg which is covered in material as dark as soot – which orbits the Sun as part of the Solar System.

Constellation An area of the night sky, often given the name of a mythical creature or character. There are 88 different constellations.

Cosmos Everything we can observe in the Universe – stars, planets and galaxies etc.

Crater A depression – shallow or deep – in a moon or planet's surface caused by the impact of a small body at high speed.

Docking The joining of one spacecraft to another. The Apollo craft docked with the Lunar lander, and the Russian *Soyuz* spacecraft docks with the *Mir* space station.

EVA – Extra Vehicular Activity Work done by an astronaut outside their spaceship, either in space in an MMU or on the surface of the Moon or another planet.

Eclipse When one celestial body passes in front of another. A solar eclipse occurs when the Moon covers the Sun.

Elliptical If the orbit of a celestial body is a smooth, oval curve instead of a perfectly round circle, it is said to be elliptical.

Equatorial Diameter The distance measured across the centre of a planet from one side to the other.

Galaxies Galaxies are vast 'islands' of many millions of stars in the dark ocean of space. Our own galaxy is called 'The Milky Way'.

Gas Giant A planet like Jupiter or Saturn, made mostly out of gas, which has no solid surface on which a spacecraft could land.

Geosynchronous Rotation When a satellite orbits a planet or moon at a certain height and moves at the same speed as the body below. It always stays above the same point on the surface.

Grand Tour The nickname given to the series of encounters made by the Voyager spaceprobes with the outer planets of the Solar System.

Greenhouse Effect When a planet's atmosphere traps the heat of the Sun near its surface and steadily raises the surface temperature.

Lander A small manned or unmanned spacecraft which descends from orbit to set down on a planet or moon's surface.

Light Year Not a length of time, but the distance light travels in one year. It is equivalent to 9.5 million million kilometres.

MMU – Manned Manoeuvering Unit A small jet back-pack worn by shuttle astronauts which lets them fly freely in space, often to capture damaged satellites.

Meteor A shooting star – a tiny piece of cometary debris which burns up in the Earth's atmosphere. Any which survive are 'meteorites'.

Milky Way The Milky Way is our home galaxy, and it contains approximately 100,000 million stars. It has a spiral shape.

Natural Satellite A planet's moon in a natural orbit, as opposed to an artificial satellite which is built by man and launched by rocket.

Nebula A cloud of dust and gas in space. Some nebulae are luminous, some reflect the light of nearby stars. Dark nebulae block the stars' light.

Nova The apparent sudden brightening of a star in the night sky. This is caused when material drawn from a companion star ignites.

OORT Cloud A theoretical shell of comets surrounding the Solar System like a bubble at a distance of approximately 1 light year.

Observatory From where an astronomer studies the night sky. It may either be a building high on a mountain or a special telescope up in orbit.

Occultation When one celestial body passes in front of another, eg. the Moon passing in front of a star.

Orbit The path of one body around another, such as the Moon around the Earth or the Earth around the Sun.

Payload Special items such as satellites and scientific equipment which are carried into space and delivered into orbit by rockets.

Phases The apparent changes of a celestial body from a thin crescent to a full disc, such as Venus, Mercury and our own Moon.

Planet A large, spherical body which orbits around the Sun or another star. Planets do not 'shine', they reflect the Sun's light.

Quasar (Quasi-stellar radio source) A highly luminous, but very distant galaxy, which was formed very early in the history of the Universe.

Radar Mapping A way of mapping a planet's hidden surface using sound waves sent from a spaceprobe or radio telescope to build up an image.

Radiation Radiation is made of electromagnetic waves or particles which travel through space carrying energy. Some forms are dangerous.

Radio Astronomy The study of radio waves coming from objects in the heavens, as opposed to the study of their light.

Radio Telescope A device shaped like a curved dish which collects radio waves from the heavens and allows them to be studied by astronomers.

Remote Control A spaceprobe is operated by remote control – commands are sent to it from operators back on Earth and it obeys them.

Retrograde Motion When a body like a comet moves around the Sun in the opposite direction to the Earth. Also, Venus has *retrograde rotation*, meaning that it spins from west to east, instead of east to west.

Ring System Millions of tiny moonlets circle the equators of the largest planets forming bands or rings. Some are bright, others faint.

Rocket Rockets launch equipment and people into space. Their engines are very powerful, enough to overcome Earth's gravity.

Shepherd Moons The tiny moons which orbit outside and inside a planet's Ring System, keeping its ring particles in place.

Solar System All the bodies – planets, asteroids, comets and moons – which orbit around our Sun. Other stars might have their own solar systems.

Space Probe A machine sent to explore a distant body with cameras and other scientific instruments controlled from Earth.

Space Station A structure of many different sections, built in orbit, where astronauts can live and work comfortably for long periods.

Spacecraft An unmanned machine sent from Earth to make measurements in space and to observe all the planets from close range.

Spaceship A manned space craft which carries astronauts into and through space and between the planets.

Speed of Light The fastest speed any object can have, equivalent to 300 million metres per second.

Star A huge, luminous sphere of hot gas sustained by internal nuclear reactions. Our own Sun is a medium-sized star.

Sun The star which lies at the centre of our Solar System. It is 109 times wider than the Earth.

Sunspots Dark, cooler areas on the surface of the Sun, caused by magnetic disturbances. They last a few weeks before dying out.

Supernova The explosive death of a massive star. This happens after it has consumed all its nuclear fuel.

Synchronous Rotation When a planet's moon takes the same time to spin once as it does to orbit its parent planet. Our Moon shows synchronous rotation so we always see the same side.

Telescope Telescopes magnify distant objects in the night sky, using lenses or mirrors to make things appear closer, bigger and brighter.

Umbra The dark centre part of a shadow. When the Moon passes within the umbra of the Earth's shadow it is totally eclipsed.

Universe The Universe is everything that exists around us – from insects to stars – whether it's been discovered or not!

Zodiac The imaginary band of the night sky, through which the Sun appears to travel during a year. The zodiac contains twelve constellations.

INDEX

Page numbers followed by the word *passim* indicate scattered mentions in the text.